"Mike is one of those exceptional CEOs who is a savvy, successful businessman that, at the same time, leads from the heart. This admirable act of balancing two, often opposing, forces is the hallmark of Mike's unique approach to leadership.

A talented storyteller who can engage others in a greater understanding of often complex economic concepts and theories while artfully drawing the listener back to how these factors influence what truly matters most to Mike—his staff and the seniors who choose retirement living as home.

I highly recommend any leader, whether new to the game or a seasoned executive, to reflect on Mike's leadership advice. I guarantee you will come away with helpful ideas on how to be even better at what we all strive to do, which is to become the very best leaders we can be."

—Cathy Hecimovich

CEO, Ontario Retirement Communities Association

"One thing that experience quickly teaches people who are willing to grow is to recognize the things you don't know. That first year for Seasons was a challenging one and we learned some important lessons that would immediately change our approach. If we wanted to establish a successful business over the long term, Seasons needed to be much more than a retirement operator. It needed to be a business that built trust so people would bring their loved ones into our communities.

My first meeting with Michael Lavallée was very refreshing, given how different his perspective was to seniors' living. I met a man who described the industry with emotion and conviction. He was passionate about his view on what needed to change in the seniors' housing sector and he taught me that Seasons was not a real estate business but rather a business built on satisfying the emotional and physical needs of our residents and their loved ones. Mike's values represented the essence of the culture we needed to create.

Michael became employee number one, and we embarked on a journey of managing our own properties and the results have been nothing short of fantastic. He continues to build a world-class team that emulates his passion and shares the same values of caring and connecting with people. Together they create an incredible culture. This culture is an extension of who Michael strives to be as a person, and we are fortunate to have him lead the team at Seasons.

—Lou Serafini Jr.
CEO, Fengate Asset Management

CONNECT, CARE, CHANGE

MICHAEL LAVALLÉE

CONNECT, CARE, CHANGE

A ROAD MAP FOR AUTHENTIC LEADERSHIP

Advantage.

Published by Advantage, Charleston, South Carolina.
Member of Advantage Media Group.

ADVANTAGE is a registered trademark, and the Advantage colophon is a trademark of Advantage Media Group, Inc.

Printed in the United States of America.

10 9 8 7 6 5 4 3 2 1

ISBN: 978-1-64225-140-1
LCCN: 2020913052

Cover design by Carly Blake.
Layout design by Mary Hamilton.

This publication is designed to provide accurate and authoritative information in regard to the subject matter covered. It is sold with the understanding that the publisher is not engaged in rendering legal, accounting, or other professional services. If legal advice or other expert assistance is required, the services of a competent professional person should be sought.

Advantage Media Group is proud to be a part of the Tree Neutral® program. Tree Neutral offsets the number of trees consumed in the production and printing of this book by taking proactive steps such as planting trees in direct proportion to the number of trees used to print books. To learn more about Tree Neutral, please visit **www.treeneutral.com**.

Advantage Media Group is a publisher of business, self-improvement, and professional development books and online learning. We help entrepreneurs, business leaders, and professionals share their Stories, Passion, and Knowledge to help others Learn & Grow. Do you have a manuscript or book idea that you would like us to consider for publishing? Please visit **advantagefamily.com** or call **1.866.775.1696**.

CONTENTS

ACKNOWLEDGMENTS

Who someone is today is the sum total of every experience they have had (good or bad) and every decision they have made in the face of those experiences.

When I considered writing this book, I wanted to use that lens to paint a picture of the lessons I had learned along my career and share some tools that I have developed along the way.

I am grateful for every single moment that has shaped me as a person. Before I even started my working career, my parents, but especially my mother, imparted the values of humility and caring for others. These values have served me well and are foundational to what this book intends to share.

As the CEO of the company that I now lead, I am also thankful for the support and partnership of our board members and of our investor, The Laborers Union of North America Pension Fund. For ten years, they supported the creation of a platform that is the genesis for this book and have given me the privilege to serve as its CEO.

This project was started in the pre-COVID-19 world we used to know.

As an organization that works in the health care industry, I can tell you that the qualities that define great leadership really shine through when faced with the incredible demands of a pandemic of this nature.

The concepts of Connect, Care, and Change are stronger than ever when lived by leaders who are making decisions and taking actions that will protect our residents and team members from illness.

I had the great privilege of seeing team members work tirelessly through months of heightened outbreak isolation protocols, and I had the sad duty of making condolence calls to family members who had lost a loved one in our care due to COVID-19.

The commitment and caring compassion that our people showed was tested by the reality that they were doing potentially dangerous work and yet they continued on their shared mission every day for our residents and for each other.

In addition to being an opportunity for inspiration, the COVID-19 pandemic has forced us all to experience loss and grief on some level. Sadly, like countless others with loved ones living in a nursing home, my mother passed away on May 1, 2020, at a time when travel between countries, provinces, and even cities was prohibited, and I didn't get a chance to say good bye prior to her passing given the emergency orders at that time.

My mother was blessed with grace, an easy laugh, and a solid wooden spoon—all of which she was happy to share freely based on what you had done to deserve them. Her wooden spoon was more a symbolic disciplinary tool, but in her hands it was effective enough. Anyone who knew her is the better for it, and I can only hope that someday the same can be said of me.

LAYING THE GROUNDWORK

How I Got Here, and Why This Book

S ometimes it's not the big, earth-shattering events that show you your path in life. Sometimes it's the little things, the quiet things. I remember the day I knew for sure that I had discovered my "calling" in the seniors housing industry.

As life-changing moments go, it couldn't have been less dramatic—at least on the surface. I was sitting in on a meeting of the resident council at a nursing home where I was serving as temporary director (a job I was eminently unqualified for). An elderly gentleman with wispy hair and reddish eyes had just been given the floor. He was holding a little notebook in his slightly shaking hand. He looked around the theater room at all the faces in attendance, cleared his throat, and said in a calm, clear voice, "Hello, my name is Elmo. Thank you for inviting me to participate in this council. I've been given the role of resident advocate for some of the more independent members of our community …"

I looked around the room and saw several jaws—belonging chiefly to staff members—literally drop open. Folks were looking at poor Elmo as if he'd just stepped out of an alien spacecraft. Why? Because only weeks earlier, Elmo had been a thorn in the side of the entire service team. He'd been labeled "disruptive," "unmanageable," and a "constant drain on staff resources." Staff had threatened to quit because of him.

Now here he was, making a positive and respectful contribution to his community.

"I've been talking to some of my fellow residents," continued Elmo, "and we've come up with a list of suggestions that we feel would improve residential life."

I felt a rush of tears to my eyes and a tightness in my throat. Elmo had changed. Profoundly. Not because of some new medication. And not because of some new clinical service the staff had provided for him (they had all but given up on him). No, Elmo had changed because of something *I* had done—I who knew almost nothing about clinical caregiving or mental health practices; I who had a degree in economics and a background in business and technology.

It was in that moment that my career path lit up for me like Montreal at Christmastime.

What had I done with Elmo that had enabled him to become happier and more productive? It wasn't rocket science, and I'll get to it in just a minute—but before I do that, you might be wondering, *How did a tech-oriented entrepreneur end up in charge of a nursing home in the first place?*

Good question. It happened almost completely by accident.

9/11 CHANGES EVERYTHING

On Friday, September 8, 2001, three days before an infamous date in world history, I was having the best damn day of my professional career, the kind of day you celebrate with caviar and champagne. My fledgling company, World English Center, had just learned that it had been greenlit for its first round of venture capital funding—$25 million for 25 percent of the company. We'd already built a great prototype product and a pathway to profitability; now we had the money we needed too. So I and my team had every reason to feel fantastic.

The VC funding hadn't come a moment too soon. I had spent the previous four years building this company and had burned through all of my personal savings, tapped out my friends and family, and pretty much exhausted the $500,000 we'd raised to get us through our early days. Now we needed the help of the institutional investment community. And we'd received it—from a company called Remington Venture Capital.

Our business? A dotcom poised to disrupt the language training industry. We were planning to deliver ESL (English as a second language) lessons in a way that had never been done before. Our model was similar to what Rosetta Stone does today—we presented language lessons over the internet and employed voice recognition and a video feedback feature to engage the user. It was an innovative way of delivering content—way ahead of the curve. A major part of our business focus was on the Asian market because that was where we saw the greatest opportunity.

Our plan wasn't necessarily to become the biggest and baddest player in the language instruction industry; our plan was to get the business rolling successfully for a few years and then sell it to a larger company and collect a nice paycheck.

So we got the commitment letter for the funding on Friday, September 8, and we couldn't have been in higher spirits. And then, literally the next business day—September 11, 2001, we were all driving to work and heard about those devastating events in New York City.

By Wednesday, September 13, we already had pretty firm indications that our funding was going to be rescinded. There were all kinds of crazy rumors flying around, including that Asia was an incubator for terrorism, and suddenly—literally overnight—no venture capitalist wanted to touch any start-ups focused on Asia. Bam. Money gone. For the next twelve to eighteen months, almost no venture capital investment took place in North America.

Long story short, we were finished. Just like that. And I was left to decide what to do next. After putting four years into building a start-up company and tapping out my own resources and my friends and family network in the process, I wasn't about to go down *that* road again, at least not for a good long while.

It looked like I was going to have to go to work for a living.

READY FOR THE NURSING HOME

I needed a job—an actual *job*. An opportunity soon arose at a family-owned nursing home business called Jarlette Health Services. They were a pretty entrepreneurial company, and I was a pretty entrepreneurial guy, so we made a good match. They didn't know the first thing about branding or marketing themselves—most nursing homes don't—so they brought me onboard to help them with that aspect of the business.

I worked on their branding for a while and also helped them with their customer service training programs. But they were growing fast and had a lot of goals they wanted to accomplish, so pretty soon it was, "Hey, Mike, we're going to be building some retirement homes; can you help us with that?" Then, "Hey, Mike, we have a construction project that could use your touch." One thing after another—and they were all challenging, interesting projects.

Early in our working relationship, they needed someone to run one of their nursing homes while the normal director was out on maternity leave. And that was how I ended up with the nursing home temp gig.

From the moment I walked in the door of Leacock Care Centre, I could see that the place was extremely clinically oriented. Here I was, a guy with a business background and zero clinical training, and now I was supposed to be leading a team of nurses and caregivers driven by clinical decision-making in a highly regulated, licensed environment? I immediately found myself … um, *challenged* by the model.

In my view, nursing homes are like any other customer service businesses. You have customers that need services, and you have staff that provide services. Simple equation. But one of the first things I noticed about Leacock was that virtually no one was focused on customer service or hospitality. Everyone was all clinical, all the time. The staff members were highly qualified, but they were working so hard to meet the medical and licensing requirements that they seemed to have no bandwidth left over for anything "extra."

The epitome of this dynamic was Heather, the clinical director. She was a well-credentialed, highly accomplished professional nurse—excellent at her job, a top-notch clinician, a good decision maker, and not a bad leader in terms of keeping staff on task. Heather's biggest challenge—the whole staff's biggest challenge—was a resident named Elmo.

Elmo, as I mentioned earlier, was very needy and disruptive to the staff's ability to care for the other residents. He would plunk himself in front of staff's work spaces and complain loudly and angrily that things were not being done properly. This happened many times a day. No one seemed to know how to manage Elmo or stop him from being such a constant disruption. From a clinical perspective, many of the staff felt he needed to be on some kind of medication to manage his behavior.

From my perspective, his needs were not clinical. They were of a different nature entirely.

Elmo's wife, I learned, lived with him at the home, and she was much frailer and less independent than Elmo was. She had complicated needs. Most of Elmo's complaints revolved around her care, directly or indirectly. His rants, it turned out, were largely attempts to advocate for *her*; they were not selfish or irrational in nature (though perhaps his expectations were unrealistic).

During one of our team meetings, early in my tenure, I said to the staff, "Elmo is our squeaky wheel. Squeaky wheels are good. They help us identify areas of the operation that are not going smoothly, and they challenge us to be better at the customer service parts of our job."

"Customer service?" countered the others. "This isn't a Carnival Cruise line. We've tried everything with Elmo. Nothing works. We can't reason with the guy."

"Fine. I'll tell you what we'll do, then," I said. "From now on, Elmo is mine. I'll take him out of your work space and engage him in a way that allows you guys to do your job."

Everyone seemed happy with that plan but dubious that things would change. But anything was better than the current state of affairs.

And so I went to Elmo and said, "The team would like me to work with you so that they can better deliver on your expectations." It was a creative interpretation of what they'd said. "So let's you and I meet every day for a while. Why don't you come see me after breakfast, and we'll talk about some of the things that are important to you."

So Elmo and I began to meet. Mostly, he would talk and I would listen. What became clear to me from day one was that Elmo was not actually dissatisfied with what the staff was doing or not doing. He was upset because he felt *he* was failing at doing what he had always done for his wife. They'd been married for sixty years, and now Elmo was no longer able to take care of her the way he wanted. She was slipping away, and so was Elmo's sense of purpose.

As our meetings went on, Elmo opened up more and more. He would come to my office in tears every day or two. It wasn't as if I was his only friend in the world. His children were around, but he didn't feel he could talk to them about how their mother was declining. He needed a confidant—someone he could talk to honestly. He also needed a sense of purpose.

One day I said to him, "Elmo, what you're really good at is being an advocate, so I'm going to give you a job. We have a resident council that meets once a month. You're one of our more independent residents. There are others who are like you and whose voice is not being heard. I think maybe these folks have some needs and wishes we're not addressing as well as we could because they haven't been speaking up. Would you be willing to be an advocate for these people? I want you to come to me with suggestions about things we could improve, and we'll do our best to implement them."

"If you think I can help, I'll give it a try," he said.

So Elmo started canvassing and interviewing his fellow residents. He was no longer "pestering" the staff every day, and when he did speak to them, he did so more respectfully. He was still struggling with the loss of his wife—who did pass away before long—but he had found a sense of purpose beyond simply caring for her. He'd also found a sense of belonging and acceptance in the community in which he lived. Leacock had finally become his home. It was a win for everyone.

So you can see why watching him speak at that resident council meeting was such a momentous event to me. A small bit of connecting and caring, a little effort to treat him like a valued customer who deserved our best service—instead of like an unwanted pest—was all it had taken to change his life completely.

I wondered how many other lives could be changed in the same sort of way.

And that was the day my vision became clear.

A NEW PATH

I had a revelation: the nursing home industry had always been great at the clinical stuff but really crappy at hospitality and customer service—and yet customer service is the real differentiator in any care-based business! It struck me that if you could be *really good* at the customer service stuff—if you could take the excellent clinical part and wrap it in a hospitality sandwich—you could create outstanding value. You could improve people's lives, and people would be willing to pay more for your services than for publicly funded settings that were strictly clinical in design. My entrepreneurial blood started flowing again.

I decided I didn't want to be in the traditional nursing home industry anymore—I didn't fit in with that clinical-first mentality—

but I did still want to serve an elder demographic, because I believed these folks were being underserved in the market.

And so I started looking at companies in the senior housing sector that were growing. Chartwell seemed to fit the bill. They were involved in a lot of mergers and acquisitions, they had recently done an IPO, and they were in high-growth mode. And so, long story short, I got myself hired by Chartwell, and that was the start of my career in senior housing.

And it was all because of Elmo and the lesson I had learned by connecting with, and caring for, that one man.

My first role with Chartwell was as associate vice president. They soon learned I was a good fixer. Whenever something was broken or they acquired a new asset, they'd have me take a look under the hood, and I would find a way to make it work. I was a good people person too. I understood how to mentor those who could be mentored while cutting loose those who could not.

So after a couple of years, I was promoted to vice president. It was a great role, but I started to realize there were drawbacks to being vice president of a publicly traded company. Doing what you need to do for the long-term good of the company is hard when you're constantly worried about the returns you're generating this month and this quarter. It's always *"Eat what you kill"* and *"What have you done for me lately?"* Your hands are tied much of the time. I found myself longing to build something from scratch—in a better way.

That opportunity finally arose. A pension fund wanted to add some senior housing assets to its portfolio, so it turned to Chartwell because of its experience in that sector. The investors came to me and said, essentially, "Mike, we want to start a new senior housing venture from scratch. Come build us a better mousetrap." I jumped on the opportunity, and that was how Seasons was born.

WHAT IS THE "SEASONS" WAY?

Seasons is a Canadian company that owns and operates thoughtfully designed retirement communities in Ontario and Alberta. I became Seasons employee number one, and the first thing I did was hire employee number two. The first question we asked ourselves was, "How are we going to do this? We don't want to be just like everybody else. We want to build a better mousetrap, but what does that even look like?"

And I said, "Everyone does what we do, so it will be our *culture* that will define us. *People* are going to provide our services, day in and day out, not you and me. No matter how great our marketing and sales are, *people* are going to have to deliver on our promises every day. The real estate part is just the envelope through which we deliver our services! Is there a company out there that knows how to build and sustain a great people-first culture?"

And the answer that came to us was, "Disney does. They're one of the most valuable brands on the planet. And they do exactly what we do. They take care of people, they serve meals, they clean rooms, they take care of properties. At the end of the day, they're us. But they do their thing in a magical-mouse sort of way, and we're going to do ours in a Seasons way.

"So let's go to Disney, let's figure out how they do it—how they hire people, how they train them, how they engrain their culture into every employee. Let's repackage that knowledge in a Seasons envelope, and let's make that model the foundation of a great business."

So that's what we did. For three years we sent our people to school at the Disney Institute in Orlando, and we told them, "You're going to bring that stuff back to us so we can repackage it."

In a nutshell, it worked. In ten years we have gone from being a company that didn't know how it was going to make payroll to one of the top twelve senior housing operators in Canada. We have 1,500 employees, we've increased our value by 390 percent, and we're still growing. Best of all, talented people want to work for us. We've become an employee magnet. And we have lots of loyal staffers who would "wear the tattoo" if we offered it.

A FANATICAL COMMITMENT TO CULTURE: THE THREE Cs

One thing we knew from the start—and Disney confirmed it a thousand times over—is that culture is everything. Peter Drucker is attributed with the quote, "Culture eats strategy for breakfast." Culture is certainly what separates a great business from a just-okay one. What Drucker was much clearer on was on results. "Results are gained by exploiting opportunities, not by solving problems."

Why is it you can walk into two different stores that sell essentially the same merchandise, and in one store you feel ignored while in the other you feel welcome and valued? Culture is the differentiator. In a great business, every employee individually exudes the values and attitudes that define the company.

But culture doesn't create itself. It must be carefully instilled and constantly reinforced so that it is well aligned with business strategy. Make no mistake: every organization has a culture, and if you don't define it, it will form on its own. It must be an integral part of the hiring process, the training process, and the day-to-day operations of the company. And the simpler your cultural values are to understand and communicate, the more likely they will stick.

> Make no mistake: every organization has a culture, and if you don't define it, it will form on its own.

It took us a while to understand that. We knew from day one that we wanted our culture to be built on people and relationships, but our first mission statements were too confusing. People had trouble repeating them back to us. Eventually we distilled our message down to three simple words that everyone could understand and rally around: Connect, Care, Change.

These are the Three Cs I learned from working with Elmo. And now those Three Cs have become the bedrock of our culture. Here's what they mean to us:

- Connect. If you're serious about making people the cornerstone of your business, then you must commit to making relationships a vital part of *what you do every day*. You must *connect*, in a heartfelt and personal way, with your customers, your employees, and your fellow management team members. Personal connection is everything. And it can't be an abstract concept, mouthed in a mission statement. It must be real.

- Care. In our company, we are all about having a servant's heart. That means caring. But caring is the one aspect of our culture that can't be taught. It's what each employee must bring to the job when they're hired and bring to work with them every day. Caring means caring for each other, for our clients, for our investors, for our image and reputation, and, yes, for the world. People don't get rich in our business, so the folks we hire need to have a moral compass that always points north and to be on a mission to make the world a better place, one person at a time.

- Change. Our customers are always evolving, and their needs are ever changing. We must be innovators so that we can continually respond to these changes. That means we can't do our job from a preconceived checklist. We know our customers can vote with their wallets, and so we must constantly compete for their hearts and minds in a dynamic way. In order for us to understand their changing needs and desires, we must always do the first two Cs: Connect and Care.

As you will see, this book—like our business—is built around those three simple concepts: Connect, Care, and Change. They are elementary ideas, but they are profoundly powerful ones. They are the magic ingredients that turn customers into raving fans and employees into lifetime partners. If you understand these three concepts and are able to model them and instill them in your staff, you will know more about how to succeed in business than any MBA graduate from Harvard or Wharton. This I promise you.

Well, you might ask, if Connecting, Caring, and Changing are such powerful and self-evident principles, then why isn't everyone embracing them? I have asked myself that question many times. Virtually every time I see a customer service business that's knocking the ball out of the park, it's because it is embodying the Three Cs. Conversely, each time I see a business that's struggling, it's because one or more of the Three Cs has been forgotten or ignored.

Many great individuals have spoken or written about the importance of culture and relationships, so why do business leaders miss such obvious concepts?

It comes down to self-awareness, I believe. Most of us don't invest the time and energy it takes to become self-aware. We tend to be task oriented. We plow through our work lives, focusing on the next task that needs to get done, day after day, without stopping to think about why we're doing what we do, how we're affecting others with our words and deeds, or how others are perceiving us.

Self-awareness, however, is the number one requirement of a successful leader. Only self-aware leaders can run self-aware businesses. A self-aware business is one that is highly conscious of the way it is affecting its customers, its staff members, its investors, and the community at large on a day-by-day, hour-by-hour basis. Great businesses that are built to last are constantly asking for feedback; they also have the cultural flexibility to respond to it. The only way you can get to a place of Connecting, Caring, and Changing—either as an individual or as an organization—is by developing self-awareness.

Hence, this book.

THE "WHY," THE "HOW," AND THE "WHO" OF THIS BOOK

Okay, so down to the nitty-gritty. The reason I wrote this book— the "why"—is to help you create a thriving business based on the Three Cs. That's why you'll notice the book is presented in three sections: Connecting, Caring, and Changing (told you, this isn't rocket science).

The "how" of the book—the way I hope to guide you to becoming a leader who is truly capable of implementing the Three Cs—is through the vehicle of self-awareness. I hope to open your eyes, not to earth-shattering new ideas, but to simple, effective, and powerful things *you* can be doing right now to build better relationships in your business.

Lastly, the "who" of the book: For whom is this book written and intended? The simple answer is *anyone in a leadership position who wants to take their business to a whole new level.* I originally planned to gear this book toward leaders of customer service–driven businesses, but then I realized: What business *isn't* customer service driven? Even if you make high-tech widgets in a strictly B2B environment, you still need to win customers and develop relationships with them. You still need to build relationships with your staff members, your leadership team, your stakeholders, and the world at large. Your brand depends on it!

No matter what kind of business you lead, learning the principles of Connecting, Caring, and Changing can be the difference maker that turns your company into a high-powered magnet for customers, employees, and investors.

Are you ready to take the leap?

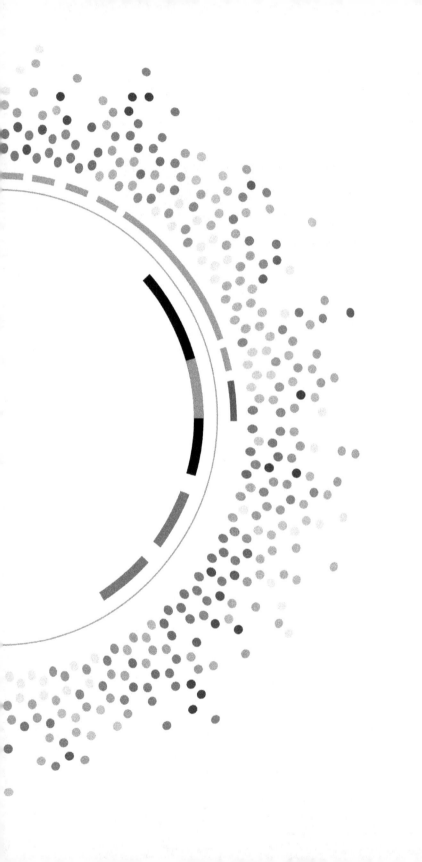

PART I:

CONNECTING

Let's talk for a moment about the idea of connecting *before we move on to the individual chapters.*

Businesses are driven by relationships. The stronger the relationships, both inside the company and outside of it, the stronger and more vibrant the business. Period.

Relationships are not passive things; they are active and dynamic. They must be tended and invigorated on a regular basis. That means we must actively connect *with the people who are important to us—all the time. Connecting means moving past the superficial "hi-how-are-yous" and making authentic contact. Connecting can include*

- *asking a coworker what they need or want,*

- *calling a customer and finding out how they're doing and what challenges they are facing,*

- *listening to an employee and asking genuine questions,*

- *sharing a laugh or a tear with others,*

- *giving a peer honest feedback,*

- *looking a customer in the eye and really seeing them,*

- *showing empathy toward a coworker,*

- *holding meetings in which all team members' thoughts are heard,*

- *and many other examples.*

How *you connect is less important than* that *you connect, and that you do so in a way that is genuine for you.*

The simple act of connecting can be profound in its consequences. And it costs nothing but a little effort. Elmo was a great example of this. We didn't invest $100,000 in his treatment or hire expensive consultants to "Six Sigma" our processes; all we did was sit down and connect with him.

I remember explaining this to the staff after Elmo's turnaround. "This was never about clinical decisions," I said to them. "It was about relationships. This job is not just about the next pill our patients need. It's about our patients' emotional happiness too, and that needs to be a big part of how we relate to them. I understand it's difficult for clinicians to make real connections with clients who die each and every day. But you have to. That's what this job requires. And I need you to go home and think about that. Because if you can't offer some human connection on top of your clinical care, then maybe this environment isn't the right one for you."

That too was an example of connecting, *by the way. It was a tough conversation, but it was a real one, and it moved us to a new place as a team.*

Relationships are complex and multilayered. We have relationships with the people we work for and the people who work for us; with the customers we serve and the vendors who serve us; with our boards, our stakeholders, our regulators, and our critics. These relationships can change at any moment too—a coworker and friend can become a direct report, an investor can become a boss. So it is vital to keep all of our relationships honest and authentic.

And it all starts with connecting …

CHAPTER ONE

AUTHENTIC CONVERSATIONS

KENDRA, A NATURAL-BORN LEADER (FOR BETTER OR WORSE)

Kendra[1] is someone I would call a natural-born leader. That doesn't mean she could walk onto a stage and give Oprah a run for her money; it just means she has the natural ability to make people like her and want to work for her.

From the time Kendra was a kid, people just seemed to gravitate toward her. She exuded an energy, an interest in things that was magnetic. On the playground, other kids wanted to play whatever

---

1   In order to provide realistic examples of the qualities and skills I want to showcase, I may use characters who are amalgams of many people. If you take a hard look within your individual organizations, you will likely find people who you associate with the ones mentioned herein. Let's take Kendra as a prime example. There is not a single person named Kendra who works in our company, but there are several Kendra personas. That's because I seek them out during our hiring practices.

game she was playing. Teachers always called on her in class. She had a natural athleticism and was always the first kid chosen for team sports or—more often—the one doing the choosing. She stood up to bullies and was admired for her self-confidence.

When it came time to elect class officers, Kendra was always nominated, even if she wasn't interested in running. She was always given larger roles in class plays than her acting talent warranted—because she had a certain presence about her.

In university, she made a lot of friends in many different social groups. She got good grades easily (except in math, for some reason), so she didn't have to try too hard. University was primarily a social experience for her, not an educational one. In her junior year she did a practicum in a nursing home, leading exercises and activities with elderly patients. Because of her natural ability to lead, she was able to motivate even the reluctant residents, and they all seemed to love her. She took a liking to this kind of work and landed a job in the recreation department of a nursing home when she graduated.

Her natural leadership talent kicked in once again. Before long, she became assistant director, then full director of a large nursing home's recreation department. Next she was promoted to a regional job where she was in charge of several homes' activity departments. Kendra hired some of her college friends to work for her, and she treated her other team members like friends too. She relied on her likability and personality as her principal management tools.

After a while things plateaued for Kendra at her job. At one point she applied for an open administrative post and was surprised when the company hired an outsider for the job. But she figured they only had bigger and better positions in store for her.

One day, the company decided to do a review of its management team. They hired a consulting firm, which came in and conducted an in-depth 360-style review. Kendra's direct reports, as well as her peers on the management team, were interviewed anonymously about her.

Kendra felt confident about the assessment process. She fully expected to receive glowing reviews from her peers and staffers and to be described as charismatic and likable; more or less the "best boss ever." She was shocked when a very different picture emerged. Her direct reports described her as lacking in empathy, "full of herself," and a poor listener. Her peers on the executive team found her to be somewhat arrogant and unreceptive to criticism.

Kendra was horrified and humbled by the feedback. She went home and proceeded to have a "dark night of the soul." She lay awake for hours, wondering how she could possibly have misjudged herself so badly. To her credit, she did not blame anyone else for her poor feedback but took the responsibility squarely on her shoulders.

She realized she had become reliant on her "charm" and was out of touch with the people around her. The very next day, she made a vow to correct that. She scheduled appointments with all of her direct reports. As she sat down with each of them, she said something to the following effect: "My recent evaluation really opened my eyes. I now see I need to do a much better job of listening to everyone on the team and finding out what's important to all of you. I need *you* to help *me* become a better manager. What things could I be doing that would help you do your job—and *like* your job—better?"

She made herself vulnerable, asked an open-ended question, and then shut up and listened. And then she listened some more. And then she scheduled more face-to-face meetings.

Her employees started opening up to her. They were hesitant at first, but then their trust began to grow. Kendra learned about the things that were important to them, their goals and dreams, their personal struggles, their ideas for making improvements to the workplace.

As she began to forge stronger connections with her people, she was able to give them vital feedback on how *they too* could improve their attitudes and performance. She became tougher on her team in many ways, but more authentic too. Whereas previously she had been concerned about being liked and being seen as everyone's friend, she now found she was more interested in helping people reach their potential.

Morale shot through the roof over the next several months, and her department was able to make a series of innovative and cost-effective changes that both the staff and residents loved. Authentic conversations had opened the door. Kendra vowed that authentic conversations would be the cornerstone of her leadership style forevermore. And she has kept that commitment.

She now views that "negative" evaluation as the best thing that ever happened to her. Twelve years later, she has earned a top leadership position at Seasons, and she sets a daily example for all as to how to have authentic conversations—with our coworkers, with our staff, with our customers. She has made a strong professional investment in developing her listening skills, her emotional intelligence, and her psychological insight, to the point where she now has the skills of a trained psychotherapist along with her seasoned management abilities. It's not something she would necessarily put on her résumé, but her counsel is valued and often sought out.

I view Kendra as a master of the authentic conversation. She is the inspiration and the source of much of the content of this chapter.

WHAT IS AN AUTHENTIC CONVERSATION?

Authentic conversations are among the most powerful tools on earth for creating a culture of connection—at all levels of a company. What do I mean by an authentic conversation? I mean one based on respect, listening, trust, and understanding—not on me telling you what to do or on preconceived outcomes.

In an authentic conversation, both parties feel heard by the other, feel free to express themselves honestly, and feel as if they are contributing meaningfully to the outcome. An authentic conversation is one in which respectful, two-way adult communication takes place, and the outcome evolves organically from within the conversation itself.

Authentic conversations are rare anywhere in the world—but especially in the workplace. Most of us tend to relate to one another, most of the time, in superficial ways that are driven by convenience and functionality. Most of our conversations are of the "Hey, how ya doin'?" or "How's that project coming along?" type. They are geared toward *avoiding* real connection and toward fulfilling our agendas.

> In an authentic conversation, both parties feel heard by the other, feel free to express themselves honestly, and feel as if they are contributing meaningfully to the outcome.

By contrast, authentic conversations allow people to connect to one another, to the company culture, and to the goals of the organization. When people are able to be authentically seen and heard by the other members of their team, they become known for who they are. And through being known, they are able to develop their potential and contribute their true talents and ideas. The organization becomes richer, stronger, and more dynamic as a result.

Authentic conversations are the core of a great culture. But they must be modeled by leadership. It's vital to have people on the leadership team who have the integrity, the courage, and the emotional intelligence to lead authentic conversations and to show managers at every level of the company how to have them too. In our organization, one of those people is Kendra.

Here are some principles, inspired by Kendra, that can lead you toward authentic conversations …

RECOGNIZE THAT WE ARE ALL ANXIETY-REDUCING MACHINES

In order to create a climate in which authentic conversations can take place, you must first recognize the role stress plays in human life. We humans are essentially anxiety-reducing machines. That is, we gravitate toward situations where we feel safe, comfortable, and relaxed, and we avoid situations where we feel threatened, attacked, and challenged. This is a natural tendency, and it can be observed in all living beings, even single-celled creatures. We embrace the familiar because we find it comforting, and we resist the unknown because it represents a potential threat to our comfort.

When stressed, our adrenal glands release cortisol—the so-called stress hormone, which serves as the body's alarm system—along with some adrenaline. And when we are faced with a threat, real or psychological, the cortisol and adrenaline force us into flight, fight, or freeze mode. We become defensive or avoidant.

The reason most of us resist authentic conversations is anxiety. An authentic conversation—one that does not follow a prewritten script—is a journey into the unknown, a detour away from our comfort zone. We don't know how the conversation is going to unfold, what new information we're going to learn, or where it's going to lead. We can't control it completely. We fear it will make demands on us that we are not willing or able to meet.

It's important, as a leader, to recognize the anxiety in yourself as well as in your team members and to do everything possible to lower the anxiety quotient all around.

From a management perspective, we tend to be anxious around the idea of confrontation. Most of us know there are issues with some of our employees, things that need to be challenged, but we don't want to call those things out because we fear the discomfort involved. It's easier to address the problems indirectly or send out memos.

On the employee side, people fear they will be criticized—or even worse, demoted or fired. They fear they will be asked to change something about the way they are currently doing their job. Change represents discomfort. Thus, even the possibility of facing criticism causes people's defenses to go up. Way up.

And so, in most conversations, both sides start "preparing their case" before the conversation even starts. And it takes very little to trigger their keyed-up defenses and shift both parties into attack/protect mode.

The key to creating authentic conversations is to do everything possible to defuse the anxiety and foster an atmosphere of open, safe, and honest two-way communication. If you don't understand the power of anxiety and avoidance, you are likely doing things that are contributing to the anxiety, not relieving it. For example …

DON'T COME LOADED FOR BEAR

Have you ever found yourself in this situation: It's a Friday afternoon. You've had a really crappy week, and it culminates in a bit of a showdown with a coworker. You stew about the encounter all the way home. You start making lists of all the wrongs the other person has committed and how that person needs to change. You start rehearsing what you plan to say to them, next opportunity. You can't do anything about it today, so you get up early on Saturday morning (you didn't sleep much anyway), pour yourself a big mug of coffee, and start writing an email to your coworker. And when you've finished itemizing all of the reasons he or she is Darth Vader and you are a Jedi beyond reproach, you fire off that email.

How do you think the ensuing "conversation" will go for you on Monday morning?

Conversation is not even the right word for what's to come. It's going to be a monologue. And what do you think is going to happen when that monologue gets rolling? Do you think the other person is going to be receptive and listen to what you're trying to say? Or are they going to shut down and go into their fight, flight, or freeze response to protect themselves from attack?

How do *you* feel when you're on the receiving end of such a monologue?

An authentic conversation cannot occur when either, or both, parties go in loaded for bear. The keys to having an authentic conversation are humility, curiosity, and openness. Before unloading on another person, *first* find out what they're thinking. Be curious rather than accusatory. And be open as to solutions. Allow ideas to emerge from within the conversation itself; don't have an end in mind before the conversation even starts.

Remember, too, that authentic conversations cannot occur when either party is in the grip of a "hot" emotion, such as anger or hurt. Allow a cooling-off period before attempting to talk.

BE VULNERABLE AND HUMAN

A tough conversation usually goes down better if it starts with vulnerability. Yours. Vulnerability builds trust and lowers people's defenses. It is a posture that *invites* the other party to open up rather than puts them on the defensive. So, for example, if you want to talk to a team member about a work problem, you might start by saying something like the following: "A few months ago, I was struggling with a personal issue, and I don't think I was doing my best work. I was hoping my boss didn't notice, and I eventually got back on track, but it was tough. Anyway, given that there's an ebb and flow to everyone's work quality, is it possible that within the last couple of months there's been an area where you haven't been giving it your best effort? And maybe something's going on that you want to talk about?"

There's a good chance they'll say no, there's nothing they want to talk about. So you just gently put it out there again: "It feels to me like something's going on, but I could be wrong."

And then you shut up, get out of their way, and listen. Nature hates a vacuum; how long do you think it will be before they begin to fill the silence? Now that you've made yourself vulnerable, do you think you will have an authentic opportunity, at some point, to shape where this conversation is going? Do you think the other person is going to be listening when you offer a counterposition or some feedback for their growth?

Letting your guard down and speaking from the heart is another essential part of being vulnerable. That means leaving the "business-speak" at the door and trying not to sound like you're reading from a company mission statement. Use normal, unpolished, everyday language.

KEEP IT BETWEEN ADULTS

Many of us, when we attain a position of authority, tend to think we need to *wield* that authority whenever possible. We lead conversations from a place of authority, especially when talking to a "subordinate."

Most conversations between management and staff tend to have this "top-down" structure. The manager sits on top and speaks down to the employee from an authority position. There's a parent-child, teacher-pupil quality to these conversations—an inherent recognition that the boss is superior to the underling.

Authentic conversations, conversely, take place between two adults. They have a lateral, or parallel, structure. They are genuine two-way conversations. Both parties have an equal voice, at least for the duration of the conversation.

There is rarely a reason to wield authority in a conversation. If you hold a higher position than the other person, that power relationship is already self-evident. Your real task is the opposite: to try to establish an egalitarian atmosphere.

It is important to remember that the position you hold in a company is simply a role you are playing at the moment. You are not inherently superior to the other person simply by virtue of your place in the company hierarchy.

In an authentic conversation, hierarchy needs to be forgotten, at least temporarily. I don't care if you're the CEO of a multinational corporation and you're talking to the night janitor. You are two human beings of equal value, and, at least for the duration of the conversation, you have equal voices. Each party accords the other adult respect.

BUILD RELATIONSHIPS

One of the main reasons for having authentic conversations is simply to get to know the people in your company (your neighborhood, your family, etc.) better. The better you know someone's life and personality, the better you can recognize when they might be facing struggles. If you know someone's values and interests, you can engage them much more easily on important topics.

And besides, it's just great to know the people you work with. You spend half your waking life at work, so why would you want to do it with people you don't know or like? A work team feels much more like family when you know and care about each other's lives.

People have a deep desire to be seen and known for who they are; it is one of the most basic human needs. A big part of any authentic conversation is simply checking in with the other person and finding out how their life is going. That means asking genuine, interested questions. The more you already know about the person, the more personal those questions can be. So it's important to make an effort to remember things about your employees' interests, families, and life circumstances.

If you don't know someone on a personal and professional level and their work starts to suffer, how will you be able to engage in the difficult conversation that says, "Hey, I noticed that you don't seem as committed to coming to work on time as you used to be. Something's changed. Is everything okay?" If the other person doesn't know you or trust you, how can you expect them to tell you, "Yeah, my marriage is falling apart," or "My husband was recently diagnosed with Hodgkin's disease?"

Only if you have a real relationship with someone can you offer them support in meaningful and unexpected ways—like saying, for example, "Listen, we have an employee assistance program. It's not something we offer to everyone, but I'm happy to be able to give you this number. No one at work will ever know you're receiving help; it's completely anonymous. No one will ever know who is accessing the support or what it is in support of. And don't worry about the bill. We pay for it."

How can you do that if you don't have a trusting relationship with someone?

BE WILLING TO HAVE THE TOUGH CONVERSATION

Of course, the stronger the relationships you create with the people in your team, the harder it can be to have difficult conversations with them. None of us like to confront a friend or a family member about a behavior pattern that is becoming problematic.

Imagine you had a friend who was in the delivery room with you when you were giving birth to your first child. Now imagine that person is your sales manager and you need to say to her, "Listen, I need you to understand something. You're getting in your own way right now. If you don't get your hands around what the problems are here, this may not be the right job for you."

That's a very tough conversation to have. It's like sitting down with your elderly dad and telling him he's no longer safe living in his own apartment and needs to move to an assisted-living program. But sometimes people need to hear difficult messages, and sometimes it's your job to tell them. Ultimately, your willingness to talk to people about the tough things is what builds authentic, long-term relationships. It's the greatest form of connecting.

Kendra is a master of the tough conversation, and she models them for the rest of us. What makes these conversations more doable for her is the genuine belief that the person she is talking to will be the prime beneficiary of the change. That's the best attitude to take. You're not asking the person to change to make *your* life easier; you're asking them to change because *they're* going to be better for it if they do. And you care about them.

We'll talk more about how to effectuate change later in the book.

AND, OF COURSE, LISTEN

By far the most important skill you can develop if you wish to have authentic conversations is the ability to truly listen. In fact, listening is such a crucial skill in connection building—and such an underappreciated skill in business—that we have devoted an entire chapter to it. So please read on.

BUT WAIT—BEFORE YOU GO!

Here are a few additional suggestions that can help you make authentic conversations an essential part of your business— and your life:

- My colleagues and I use a technique we call the "Millennial Sandwich" when having a conversation with a Millennial employee. (Millennials are the generation that was raised on "everyone gets a trophy for just showing up." Not their fault at all, but as a result, they tend to be sensitive about negative feedback.) When you want to make a critical observation of someone, sandwich it between two compliments. It works on everyone, not just Millennials!

- Something I learned from marriage: if you're carrying around stress or anger, find a way to "safely" vent it before attempting a productive conversation. In a marriage, for example, you might tell your spouse, "I just need to blow off some steam about something that happened at work. It'll just take a few minutes. Then you and I can have a nice dinner together."

- "I" statements are much less abrasive than "you" statements. Instead of saying, "You've really been dropping the ball lately," try saying something like, "I notice myself feeling less confident about your work lately." When you hurl an accusation at someone, their defenses shoot up, and their impulse is to argue with you. When you simply report your own experience or feeling, no one can argue with you.

It takes time to establish a culture in which authentic conversation is the norm, but if you consistently model, encourage, and support this type of communication, it will grow roots.

CHAPTER TWO

THE ART OF LISTENING (INPUT)

I n order to have authentic conversations—and create a culture of Connection—you must be skilled at both the *output* (sending) side and the *input* (receiving) side of communication. Oddly, most businesses, and people, focus 90 percent of their energy on the output side—talking, writing, presenting—and very little on the input side—listening.

That formula needs to be reversed. Listening is absolutely *foundational* to great culture, not a side consideration. The art of listening shapes and underpins all authentic communication. That is why we have devoted an entire chapter to it. We could have made it an entire book.

A TALE OF POOR LISTENING

Early in my senior housing career, I was an associate VP responsible for a number of properties. One day I was meeting with my supervisor, the COO, and we were discussing my "problem child"—a home that was not well positioned in the market and struggling with its marketing and sales initiatives. Its occupancy was lagging as a result. My boss and I raised the possibility of changing the home's service model from an all-inclusive, one-price-for-everything operation to more of a debundled, à la carte sort of model.

One thing we realized during our conversation was that Ellen, the manager of the property in question, would probably not be very receptive to such a change. Nor would she be hugely effective at implementing this new type of service model. So how should we handle her? That was the question. Ellen was nearing her retirement age, so that was a consideration too.

Not long after my conversation with the COO, I scheduled a site visit to the property Ellen managed. My mind was locked and loaded on implementing a new strategy to improve this home's business model. So I sat down with Ellen and dived right in.

"What do you think," I asked her point-blank, "about changing to a service model where we layer in self-serve and create more of a buffet-style operation? Is that something you would be able to champion and execute?"

Ellen looked at me as if I'd thrown hot coffee at her. Her response, not surprisingly, was, "Gee, that's not our reputation. That's not something we've done before. It would require a completely different staffing model. I don't think it would be successful."

I forged boldly ahead: "Well, what if that was the decision we made at the head office? Would you give it a shot? Would you stick around? Or would you see it as an opportunity to let someone else take leadership so you could retire? Oh, and by the way, what *are* your retirement plans?"

Ellen seemed rather stunned by my questions, so I left them hanging for the moment. My thinking was that, since she was my direct report, she would think about her answers and get back to me. But a few days later, I received a phone call from my COO, who was … not pleased.

"Did you have a conversation with Ellen last Friday?" he asked, his voice spring-loaded with tension. "And did you bring up that à la carte idea you and I discussed?"

"Yes," I replied.

That was the one and only word I uttered in that entire "conversation."

My boss proceeded to tear me a new … um, earhole. "What if I told you I've been on the phone all morning," he barked, "with people telling me how awful it was for you to try to push Ellen out of her job?"

I tried to explain that I had not tried to push Ellen out, but I never got the chance to speak. The conversation became nothing but a shouted monologue. "You had no authority to move forward with this initiative!" thundered the COO. "What the hell were you thinking? What gave you the right to leap from a strategy discussion right to the implementation stage? If you ever 'go rogue' on me like that again, I will *eviscerate* you. Do you hear me? From now on, I want to know every fuckin' move you make before you do it …" On and on it went in that vein.

The call ended with a click and a hang up. My heart was racing from adrenaline overload. A minute later, my phone rang. A colleague.

"Hey, Mike, are you okay?" he timidly queried.

"Yeah," I lied. "Why?"

"Because everyone on the third floor heard that smackdown. Wow."

Yes, the verbal assault had been so vicious my colleagues *had to check on me to make sure I was okay.* That call permanently altered my relationship with my boss, and it also became a defining moment for me. I realized this was the kind of leader I never wanted to be. If my boss had taken just a moment to listen to me, the situation could have been resolved in a positive way. Instead it had devolved into an emotional tirade at my expense.

But after licking my wounds, I thought about the incident some more and realized I was not blame-free. Far from it. My own failure to listen, both to my boss and to my direct report, had set the whole train wreck in motion. The COO was right: I had leaped from a strategy discussion stage to the implementation phase without warrant. And Ellen was right in feeling like I was trying to push her out. After all, I'd ambushed her with an idea that I had already worked out in my head and had not taken the time to listen to her response.

Here is how all three of these communication breakdowns could have been handled a little more wisely:

My boss, first of all, should have cooled off before attempting any sort of communication with me. And he should have asked me to come to his office *in person.* Ideally, he should have focused the lens on himself before jumping to accusations. For example, he could have said, "Thinking back on our conversation, I'm wondering what *I* said or did to convey the notion that it was okay for you to move on to implementation. How did I fail to create clarity in our talk?" And then he could have sat back and listened to my response, openly and nondefensively.

For my part, where *I* messed up in my initial conversation with my boss was in failing to listen for his intentions and checking back with him to make sure he and I were aligned. As soon as we started talking about Ellen, my mind jumped to, "Ellen is a problem that must be solved ASAP." Mentally, I leaped straight to the solution phase (a bad habit of mine) and was no longer listening to him. At the end of the conversation, I should have checked in with him and told him I was planning to talk to Ellen. Taking that step would have corrected for my earlier failure to listen and would have stopped me from going off half-cocked as I cheerfully did.

Finally, when I was talking to Ellen, I should have *explored* the idea of switching service models with her in a more open-ended, informational way rather than presenting it as a plan already on the table. And I should have taken the time to really listen to her ideas. Instead I went directly into "consensus-building" mode and had only two possible outcomes in mind: (1) you're going to commit to my idea and try it, or (2) you're going to admit you don't want to try it and retire.

Unsurprisingly, she could smell my agenda from a mile away, and she felt threatened by it.

Three opportunities for better listening—three swings and misses. Had any one of these listening opportunities been handled better, an ugly outcome could have been avoided, and relationships could have been improved.

Opportunities like this present themselves *every single day* within *every single organization*. And in virtually every instance, optimizing those listening opportunities will make your culture—not to mention your bottom line—stronger.

Let's take a deeper dive into the "listening cycle," from how to seize and create listening opportunities to how to maximize the input we receive.

SHIFT INTO "LISTENING GEAR"

One simple step can alleviate the majority of listening failures that arise in business and life. That is to learn to recognize *opportunities to listen*, to seize them, and to consciously shift into "listening gear." Listening is a very different mental activity from lecturing or problem solving. In order to shift into listening gear, you must be clear on what listening really is.

Listening is not about learning how to politely take turns while conversing. It is not about "being patient" or "holding your tongue" while another person is speaking so that you can silently rehearse what you're going to say next. It is not about nodding and acknowledging the other person's ideas so that you can refute them one by one or offer immediate solutions.

> The goal of listening, plain and simple, is to *learn*; to better understand another human being. Simply that and nothing more.

The goal of listening, plain and simple, is to *learn*; to better understand another human being. Simply that and nothing more. We listen so that we may learn who another person is, what they think and feel, and what is important to them. Listening is an act of discovery.

Unfortunately, this is not the way conversation is modeled for us in the media, where the chief rule seems to be, "The person who talks the loudest and listens the least shall be deemed the 'winner.'" Actual *listening*—and, God forbid, changing your mind based on what the other person is saying—is often portrayed as a form of weakness.

We need to lose the idea that a conversation is a contest to be won or an agenda to be sold. A conversation, rather, should be an adventure in opening up and learning. And as such, it requires a shifting of mental gears. The moment we sit down with someone to have a conversation—or when a conversation spontaneously occurs—we need to take a conscious pause and remind ourselves why we are listening: to gather input, not to advance our output.

If you are a natural listener, you do this step automatically. If you are not, then learning to take this simple gear-shifting step can save your business, your career, and your relationships.

Step one: engage listening gear. It's critical.

ENGAGE

In order to listen, of course, you must get the other person to talk. That begins with the simple act of engagement. As I've said before, I remind my employees (and myself) over and over again how powerful the simple act of engagement can be. Focusing on our job duties should never be an excuse not to engage with customers and coworkers and to listen to what they have to say.

I was schooled on this principle myself some years back. One day I was visiting one of our properties with the goal of implementing a specific change that I was sure would improve life for the residents. And I was *on task*. I had a piece of paper in my hand and was walking by the in-house bistro where these two elderly gentlemen were sitting. Remember the grumpy old men from *The Muppet Show*? These two guys could have played those roles.

Well, as I walked by them, one of them leaned toward the other and said, "Look at that fucker. So damn self-important. We pay his salary, and he can't even lift his head and say hello."

Overhearing them (as I'm sure was their intention), I stopped in my tracks, turned to them, and said, "I apologize. First of all, my name's Mike."

"We know who you are; you're the guy who raises our rent."

39

I let the remark pass. "I apologize, because you're right," I said to them. "I should never be so busy or self-important that I can't take the opportunity to say hello. Would you mind if I sat down and had a coffee with you in a few minutes?"

They said fine.

So … after quickly finishing up the task I was on, I returned to the table, and we had coffee together, and I listened to them. They actually had a lot of positive things to say—to my surprise. From that point on, whenever I showed up at that property, they would expect me to stop and have coffee, and they would share their thoughts with me—what they liked and didn't like about the residence. They became my squeaky wheels, my new Elmos. I received immensely valuable customer feedback and "intel" from these two gentlemen. I also formed a human bond with them over time, and they transformed from "enemies" to allies.

The mistake I'd made on that first day was in trying to jump straight to Change without doing the steps of Connect and Care. My grumpy old men taught me a lesson: You must take the time to connect with the people around you by engaging them. And if you listen, they will talk.

And you will learn.

QUESTION PRODUCTIVELY

If you want people to open up, you must learn to ask them questions that go beyond the "Hey, how are you?" or "Did you order this weather?" variety. You must get past the superficial. Three principles I have learned in this regard are the following:

- Ask open-ended questions. An open-ended question is one that requires more than a one-word or a yes-or-no response. Open-ended questions stimulate "essay" answers rather than "fill in the blank" answers. They get people talking. Examples of open-ended questions include "What are your ideas about this new policy?" or "What were the best things you did on your vacation?" An open-ended question says, *I am giving you space to talk so that I may listen.*

- Lead with the positive. When I sat down with my grumpy old men, the first thing I asked them was, "Can you tell me what you like about living here?" I did this not for my own comfort but for theirs. People generally find it easier to offer positive commentary than criticism. Why? Because they know *you'll* be more receptive to it. So it's usually wise to allow people to start on a positive note. If you demonstrate that you can listen thoughtfully to their positive comments, they'll develop trust in you and feel more comfortable sharing their critical thoughts.

- Keep it personal. Ask people about *their* lives, *their* relationships, *their* dreams, *their* goals. Listen to their answers and remember them. Every human being has a desire to be known and heard. Be the person people can talk to about themselves, and you will be a friend forever.

The main goal of asking conversational questions is not to ascertain factual data but to open people up and learn more about them as people.

RESPECT THE POWER OF SILENCE

Great listeners understand and utilize the power of silence. They know that nature hates a vacuum and that silence creates an empty vessel into which information can flow. Most people are uneasy with silence, especially in social situations, and will usually try to fill it up. So if you want someone to talk, provide them with silence, and watch what happens.

Silence is the tool police investigators use to get people to spill the beans during interrogations. They know that if they sit there and remain silent long enough, the suspect or witness will start talking just to relieve the discomfort. And if the "person of interest" talks long enough, new pieces of truth will begin to emerge.

The trick to learning to use silence effectively is to get over *your own* discomfort with it so that you don't start reflexively filling the silence yourself. Let the *other person* fill it. Ask an open-ended question and then shut your nutcracker. Let the magic happen.

In a mysterious way, silence seems to evoke truthfulness. Direct questioning can put people on the defensive and stimulate guarded responses; silence, on the other hand, is open ended and nonthreatening. Perhaps that is why churches, temples, libraries, courtrooms, and monasteries are places of silence.

Make silence a principal tool in your listening tool belt.

PRACTICE ACTIVE LISTENING

Once the other person starts speaking, use active listening techniques to keep the flow of conversation going and show the person you are fully engaged. A few key aspects of active listening include the following:

- Be conscious of sending and receiving nonverbal cues. Use alert and attentive body language when someone else is speaking. Sit forward in your seat. Don't slouch. Make frequent (but not constant) eye contact. Nod. Smile when appropriate. From time to time, mirror the other person's body language to help them feel more relaxed.

Also, be aware of the messages your body language is sending. Crossing your arms and leaning back signals defensiveness. Pursing your lips says "I'm holding my tongue." A furrowed brow indicates disagreement or confusion. Try to signal noncritical openness and receptivity.

Also pay active attention to the body language the other person is using. Do they appear guarded, relaxed, angry, tired? If so …

- Share your observations. If the other person seems uncomfortable, distracted, or reluctant to speak, share your observation in nonaccusatory way: "I get the sense there's more you want to say about that," or "I'm feeling you're not really comfortable right now. Am I wrong?" Use "I" statements when doing this so you don't sound accusatory.

- Reframe and restate. At frequent intervals, repeat back what you believe the other person is saying but using your own words. At the end of the conversation, check in with the person and summarize what you think you heard from them.

- Stay present. Keep your focus on the other person. Curtail your inner dialogue. Silence your phone, and turn off any distracting sights and sounds. If you notice yourself "mentally rehearsing" what you're going to say next, shift gears back to listening mode.

REFRAIN FROM JUMPING IN

When you are listening, your job is to receive input. Period. That means you must resist the temptation to interject and interrupt.

There are several reasons we tend to jump in on other people before they have fully said what they need to say. Some of these reasons are that we want to correct something the person said, we want to argue with them, we want to provide solutions, or we want to interject our own story. It is natural, and even okay, to do some of these things on occasion, but it is wise to be aware of our interruption tendencies and to work on reducing them.

For example, I've been told many times in performance appraisals, "Mike, you jump to conclusions before people are done giving you the facts. You're very solution minded." I've had to work on my tendency to jump to solutions and have become a better listener as a result.

Generally, the only *good* reasons to jump in on others are to clarify a point you don't understand, to offer them encouragement to go on, to show understanding, or to gently guide them back on track when they have wandered off the topic.

LIFT YOUR ANCHORS

To be a good listener, you need to be aware of what I call your "anchors." We all have them. These are beliefs, entrenched positions, or ideas that are central to our particular world view or our view about various aspects of business. We tend to pull conversations in the direction of our anchors because it makes *us* more comfortable to do so. But if we want to become good listeners, we must lift our anchors and let the "ship of conversation" flow freely. That means being open to new ways of seeing things and curious about how others see the world.

DIFFICULT LISTENING SITUATIONS

There are times when listening becomes a challenge, either because the other person is expressing a strong negative emotion or because the other person is lying. How do we handle these situations as good listeners?

Strong emotions, such as anger and sadness, tend to push our buttons. When someone is expressing anger or complaining, we tend to want to defend ourselves or argue back, and when someone is expressing grief or fear, we want to "fix" it. The worst thing you can do when someone is expressing strong emotion is to argue or fix it. Rather, let the person express their emotions fully, then be as empathetic as possible and appropriate.

Lying represents a special challenge. It is difficult to listen empathetically when you sense the other person is trying to manipulate or deceive you. The best thing you can do is uncritically allow the person to talk, and when they are finished, ask probing, nonthreatening questions around any inconsistencies you noted. Reframe and restate the facts until more of the truth comes out, and then say something like, "If this is the real truth, I'm wondering why you felt you had to start out where you did." Try to be introspective rather than accusatory. Ask yourself—and the other person—"Is there anything *I'm* doing that makes you feel you can't be truthful with me about this topic?"

FOLLOW-UP: THE MAGIC SAUCE

After you have listened to someone, the surest way to prove to them that you truly heard them is to follow up later on. The next time you see the person, ask questions like, "Remember when you said [x] wasn't going so well? How's that been since I last saw you?" If the person gave you critical feedback about yourself, show them you heard them by demonstrating adjusted attitudes and behaviors. If they made legitimate complaints or suggestions about the business, show that you heard them by making some changes.

Follow-up is the magic sauce that proves listening took place and builds trust for future communications. Follow-up closes the communication loop beautifully.

BUT WAIT—BEFORE YOU GO!

Here are a few additional suggestions that can help you build great listening into your personal repertoire and your culture:

- Listening is not done with the ears only. It is a whole-body, whole-mind experience. The eyes are an essential part of listening. So is the heart.

- Ninety-nine percent of conflicts within an organization can be defused, if not completely resolved, by *listening* to all the parties involved and making them feel fully heard.

CHAPTER THREE

CONNECTIVE COMMUNICATIONS (MASTER YOUR OUTPUT)

L istening is the foundation of the Connect principle. You can't connect to others if you don't know who they are and what they care about. That means you must gather input from them. Of course, output is critical too. What *you* have to say is essential. But you must learn to offer your output in such a way that it is *received as input* by others rather than ignored or rejected.

As a leader, your job by definition is to influence people—customers, *prospective* customers, frontline staff, managers, stakeholders—and to get them all rowing in the direction you wish. Many leaders try to do this by brute force—by "issuing edicts" and expecting people to follow them: "Here's the way we're going to do things from now on ..."

Authoritative communications are extremely crude and ineffective, however, and should be seen as a last resort. They raise people's defenses and cause them to double down on their previous positions. To influence people in a productive, positive, and effective way, you must create *connective* communications. You must build bridges to other people via all the various types of output you send.

MISSED CONNECTIONS

Every day presents virtually limitless opportunities to either connect with people through our words and actions or to divide and alienate them. Speaking for myself, I haven't always seized connection opportunities in my career. Here's an example of a "missed connection" on my part.

A few years ago, when I was still COO at Seasons, we bought a group of residences in Alberta, and I and our executive VP were responsible for managing direct relationships with the new residential communities. So we were going around doing town halls with all of our new residents in order to introduce ourselves and our company to them. The general thrust of these group meetings was, "Welcome to the family. We're extremely happy to be able to serve you. Here's what you can expect from us, and here's what you shouldn't be worried about."

One day I was giving my intro spiel to the residents of one of our new homes, and I was on the topic of who was going to take care of serving dinner and cleaning their suites. A lovely lady from Alberta raised her hand, stood up, and said, "I hope you don't expect to bring all of your construction workers from Ontario to come and take our Alberta jobs."

O-kay.

The remark had come entirely out of left field. I hadn't been talking about anything construction related, and so I kind of chuckled (a bit superiorly, perhaps) in response. She snapped, "I'm serious, young man," and folded her arms in accusation.

Now I felt *my* defenses rising up. "I have no idea where this remark is coming from," I said to her, "but let me just explain the economics of a scheme like you're suggesting. If I decided to bring busloads of people from Ontario to Alberta to build or renovate buildings, wouldn't that be tremendously expensive? I'd have to offer them relocation incentives, I'd have to pay their transportation, I'd have to put them up in hotels, and I'd have to pay their wages as well. Wouldn't that be a costly business proposition? And to what end? If there are good tradespeople to hire here—as I assume you believe there are—why would I want to bring workers from Ontario to do what can be done more cost effectively here?"

Bam. Game, set, match. I had won the point with my irrefutable logic.

So why didn't I feel like a winner? When I looked out on that small sea of faces, I could see that I had won absolutely no one over to my side. Rather, I had pushed them further away. Etched on every face in that room was the sentiment, "You're from Ontario, and we hate everything from Ontario, including you now." It didn't matter how airtight my arguments were. I had made the crucial mistake of trying to influence people without connecting with them first. Now I was going to have to do damage control.

What I *should* have done is lead with a remark such as, "Oh, by the way, I know you guys probably think people from Ontario don't understand the realities of what happens in Alberta. So let me tell you, I grew up in an Alberta community as an army brat. We lived in Cold Lake for several years when we moved from our first posting in Germany ..."

If I had opened with that story, it would have defused the "Alberta versus Ontario" animosity. It would have created immediate credibility and an immediate connection as well.

ARISTOTLE WAS RIGHT

You see, there is more to influencing people than simply being right. A long time ago, Aristotle figured out that if you want to be an influencer, you must succeed on three levels: *logos*, *ethos*, and *pathos*. It's not enough to impart good information (logos); you must also come across as credible and authentic (ethos), and you must connect to people in an empathic way (pathos).

An effective communicator always works on all three levels.

Briefly, here's what I mean by the three levels, framed in more contemporary language:

- Logos = Agility. By agility, I mean the mental ability to get a good read on situations and to propose effective ways to get things done. Agile leaders can analyze strategies and evaluate facts and risks on the ground. They can incorporate lessons learned in the past and present ideas in a logical and compelling fashion.

- Ethos = Authenticity. Authentic communicators are able to establish personal credibility with their audience. They possess some form of "credentials" relative to the subject matter, and they also speak from the heart, openly and honestly. Authentic communicators speak to dreams, visions, and aspirations. They inspire hope for the future.

- Pathos = Empathy. Empathic communication is based on making an effort to understand the party you are speaking to. It evidences caring, a willingness to see people as people, not just as resources for accomplishing tasks. It is based on relationship building.

Here are the three communication levels in a bit more detail:

AGILITY (LOGOS)

To communicate with agility means to have your case well thought out and to "get it right." It means to provide your listener(s) with logic, statistics, expert opinions, and historical facts and to appeal to their reasoning ability and common sense. A good trial attorney tries to win a case using chiefly logos (with a liberal dash of ethos and pathos thrown in).

More than just knowing the argument you want to present, however, you must also know your audience. What is their general background, training, age, education level, and so on? What do they have in common with each other (if you're talking to a group)? What do they have in common with you? What is their likely reaction to the material you are trying to communicate? Might they be defensive, suspicious, skeptical? Are there cultural, professional, or geographic factors to consider? How would you feel if you were in their shoes? These are questions I failed to consider before talking to my Alberta residents.

To be an agile communicator also means to be prepared. Anticipate the kinds of questions you might be asked, and have good answers ready. Be prepared to explain difficult or complex concepts in a clear and simple way. Have an "elevator pitch" ready—that's the ten-second version of your concept that anyone can understand.

At Seasons, we have a communications specialist who helps us prepare in an agile way. She provides us key information in digested chunks, such as, "Here's the goal. This is who these people are. Here's what they want to know. Here are some sample questions you need to be prepared to answer, and here are the key messages you need to deliver." She doesn't feed us words to parrot; she just makes sure we're prepared to stay on message if someone sticks a microphone in our face. It's one way that we stay good at the agility (logos) game.

If you've followed any political campaigns or debates, however, you know that being armed with convincing facts and sound bites is not enough to win elections. You need to connect to people on the other levels as well.

AUTHENTICITY (ETHOS)

If you want to influence people, they must trust you as a source. They must believe that you have the experience, credentials, and/ or authority to impart the information you are sharing and to relate to them as an audience. There must be a foundation of trust. Had I taken the time to tell my Alberta audience that I had lived in Alberta for years, I would have been seen as a trustworthy source instead of a hostile outsider. And an authentic conversation could have taken place.

We spent a chapter talking about authentic conversations, so I won't repeat that material here, but one additional aspect of authentic communication that is essential to consider is language. The language with which you communicate your message(s) must feel authentic to the people to whom you are speaking.

Some companies like to create their own special jargon as a way of connecting with their team members. Departments within companies tend to use specialized jargon as well. Nurses, for example, speak to each other in a specific shorthand way, as do IT people. As an executive, I tend to speak in terms of financial performance or high-level KPIs—things that are important to me from a management perspective.

In most situations, though, I think a plainspoken, brown-bread approach is generally best. If I were to speak to a frontline employee whose job is to clean floors about "net profit margins" and "debt-to-equity ratios," the person would look at me as if I were a well-dressed lamp. So I try to speak in everyday, brown-bread language, enabling connections to form.

You can speak in specialized jargon within your own silo without losing authenticity, but when you communicate outside your own discipline, it's important to use a language everyone can understand. Otherwise, authenticity is lost, even if you're speaking honestly.

At the same time, you need to respect everyone's intelligence and not create the impression that you are talking down to anyone. That's why, when I'm speaking to larger groups or in situations where a certain amount of gravitas or professionalism is needed, I may use somewhat higher-level language. But even when I do this, I will often stop to clarify a technical-sounding term to make sure everyone is with me—"That's just a fancy way of saying we need to balance our checkbook every month."

When in doubt, speaking from the heart, not the head, is usually the best guidance.

EMPATHY (PATHOS)

Finally, the real secret to influencing people with your communications is to connect with them empathically. That is, to understand who they are as human beings—what they struggle with, what they are fearful of, what is important to them. Empathic communications are not merely *transactional*—do A for me, and I'll do B for you—they are *relational*. They are based on having genuine human relationships with the people you are addressing.

Pathos also speaks to the importance of emotions. People connect to one another through their emotions, not their intellect. Also, people are *moved to action* by their emotions. It doesn't matter how convincing your ideas are if people are unmoved by them. You must connect to people on an emotional level if you want to move them to a new place.

By far, the most potent tool for connecting to people on an emotional level is storytelling ...

STORYTELLING, THE MASTER TOOL

If you want your messages to connect with people, you must embrace the power of the story. Human beings are storytellers by nature. The way we make sense of our own lives, and the world around us, is through telling stories. The way a company communicates its mission, its culture, and its values is also through storytelling. Storytelling is the master tool of messaging.

> As a leader, *you* must control the storytelling mechanism of your organization. You must tell the stories *you* want to tell about your company.

As a leader, *you* must control the storytelling mechanism of your organization. You must tell the stories *you* want to tell about your company. Because stories *will* be told, one way or another. In the absence of compelling stories from *you* about your company, people will invent their own stories. Your job is to tell better stories than the rumor mill can generate.

Great communicators have always known the power of storytelling. Today, science is confirming that power in new ways. We now know, for example, that stories synchronize a listener's brainwaves with those of the storyteller through a process known as *neural coupling*. FMRI studies show that storytelling "lights up" sections of the brain that factual information does not.[2] Storytelling enhances memory and improves attention.[3] It can even change the brain's chemistry through the release of oxytocin.[4] Evidence shows people are more likely to donate to a cause or buy a product after seeing an emotionally stirring story about it.[5] The list goes on.

At Seasons, we pay a lot of attention to storytelling. We are constantly looking for ways to capture stories about our residents and staff members that reflect some aspect of our Connect, Care, Change culture. It is so much easier to communicate these concepts through stories than through explanations. One of our main goals at Seasons, for example, is to create what we call *meaningful moments* with our residents every day. We like to tell the stories of these meaningful moments whenever and wherever possible.

Recently, as a way to encourage the creating and sharing of these moments, we started a contest to reward the employee who had the best "meaningful moment" story to tell. We decided that one winning employee in Ontario and one in Alberta would receive the prize of a trip to Disney World worth up to $10,000. In Ontario, we had one participant—we'll call her Jean—who told a wonderful story, but then another person in the same home—call her Ellen—also told a

---

2   Thu-Huong Ha, "What happens in the brain when we hear stories? Uri Hasson at TED2016," TED Blog, February 18, 2016, https://blog.ted.com/what-happens-in-the-brain-when-we-hear-stories-uri-hasson-at-ted2016/.

3   "Why Storytelling Works: The Science," Ariel, updated November 30, 2017, https://www.arielgroup.com/why-storytelling-works-the-science/.

4   Ibid.

5   Ibid.

great story. But as Ellen was telling her story, she stopped and said, "You know, as much as I would like this prize for my own family, you have to reward Jean, and here's why."

And then Ellen proceeded to tell a story about what an exceptional person Jean was—baking cookies at home for the residents, coming in on her day off to create a picnic for the Memory Care residents, and more. After listening to both stories, we said, "Crap, we have a problem. Jean *should* win and needs to win. But Ellen also needs to win, because she embodies exactly the same qualities and is also selfless." So we ended up having two Ontario winners instead of one.

And then we realized, "Hey, *that in itself* is a great story!" So now we're going to tell the story of the two Ontario winners to all of our employees at our annual conference, through a videotaped presentation. There won't be a dry eye in the house, least of all my own. And it's all because we're always seizing opportunities to tell stories.

Storytelling, as you can see, is not just about the company telling stories to its employees; it's about giving employees the opportunity to share their own stories. People love to *tell* stories as much as to hear them, and they will tell amazing stories about your company culture—if you give them the opportunity to do so. Capture those stories and share them—in your printed materials, on your website, at meetings and conferences—whenever and wherever you can.

COMMUNICATE ON MANY LEVELS

To create and maintain meaningful connections with your employees and customers, you must continually communicate with them in as many ways as possible—across a variety of mediums and in a variety of ways.

At Seasons we have a number of channels for that. For example, twice a year, we issue a printed publication for our staff in which we tell them how things are going and some of the great things we've accomplished as a team. We also create videotaped messages, about once a quarter, from our team leaders to their teams. These are viewable through our payroll portal, where everyone needs to go to get their pay stubs.

Here are a few additional methods we use to communicate meaningfully with our people …

TOWN HALLS

Town halls are a vital way in which management and frontline staff interact and communicate. We use them to reinforce our culture, celebrate our accomplishments, make changes, and set our sights on future goals. We start each town hall by offering a "state of the union" presentation—how we're doing as a company. Then usually we share one bright idea that has been contributed, often at the previous year's town hall, and show how it evolved into a real policy or procedural change.

And every year we ask the question, "If we could do one thing differently that would make your job better, what would that look like? What obstacles can we remove that are getting in your way?" We usually get some productive responses. Sometimes an offered idea is one that may be challenging to implement, so we open a dialogue about it. Whether or not we ultimately decide to implement the idea, we have an authentic conversation about it. And that alone has immense value.

"TEN AT TEN" HUDDLES

Every morning at ten o'clock, our team leaders have what we call "huddles," where they do some cultural messaging and discuss whatever is topical for the day so that everyone on staff knows what's going on and is on the same page. So, for example, if there is a resident who is a little confused that day, we'll alert the team to that. Later, if that resident asks a staff member what time it is, the employee will be prepared to say, "Well, Mrs. Smith, it's twelve fifteen. Almost time for lunch. We're having pot roast today, and the chef says it's going to be especially good." Via that small interaction, the staff not only helps to orient a resident who might be mixing up lunchtime and dinnertime but also creates an event the resident can look forward to.

The idea is for the whole staff to be grounded in what is going on operationally that day and also to be motivated and prepared to live the culture. Huddles are one of our chief communication tools. They're mandatory, and we take notes so that everyone in subsequent shifts will know what took place during the day.

REAL-TIME FEEDBACK

At Seasons, we don't believe in doing annual performance reviews for hourly employees. We think giving timely feedback, good or bad, is better than saving up all our feedback for that one day where we tell you whether you've earned a three, a four, or a one out of four. One way we provide positive real-time feedback is to place service flags on people's name tags. These flags are awarded for showing excellence in key service areas such as presentation, safety, and efficiency.

During our "ten at ten" huddles, we allow team members to nominate each other. In front of their coworkers, we award these individuals with service flags so as to say, "Here's an example of what safety looks like." It's a reaffirmation of our committed goals, and it also stimulates storytelling. For example, a resident might stop a staff member and say, "Irene, what's that blue thing on your name tag?" And Irene will say, "My teammates thought I did a great job preparing the tables for the holiday lunch today." In telling that little story, the employee makes a connection with a resident and also reinforces how important service is to us.

On the flip side, if someone is off their game in some way, our service team leaders are trained to provide coaching on the spot, or as soon as possible. So, if I walk into a home and I see someone's not wearing their name tag, I will take them aside and say, "Hi, I'm Mike. I don't see your name tag on. Did you lose it this morning?" And if they say, "I forgot it," I might say, "Let's go make one for you right now at the front desk, because it's important for the residents to know who you are." Then I might go to their service team leader and say, "I just mentioned to Joanne that she didn't have her name tag. Did you guys notice that at the ten at ten?"

So, this interaction becomes an opportunity to coach the service team leaders too. Coaching interactions are recorded in employee records, so that if further instances of the problem behavior occur, we can identify the need to take additional steps.

NONVERBAL COMMUNICATIONS

We also strive to better connect with our customers through the nonverbal communications we offer. These include things like the pictures we hang on the walls, the way we plate the meals in the bistro, and even the uniforms the staff wear. *What do uniforms have to do with communication?* you might ask.

Quite a bit, actually. When we bought the portfolio of homes in Alberta, for example, all the various teams wore different uniforms, as is typical in most companies. We told the staff we were thinking of changing the uniforms and asked for their feedback about this.

"We think our team should wear blue uniforms," suggested the nursing team.

"We think our team should continue to wear red," said the dietary team.

To this I replied, "Why?"

They answered, "So we can look distinct from other staff."

I said, "Hmm, so if there's a resident who has a spill on their floor, they'll think, 'I won't talk to the people in blue—they can't solve my problem. I won't talk to the people in red—they can't solve my problem. I need someone in housekeeping.' And then they'll have to wait for a green uniform to show up or go looking for someone. So, by the color of your uniform, you've made it harder for the resident to ask for the service they need. How is that good for them?"

Everyone went silent. I continued, "It doesn't matter how good the care is here; if the room isn't clean, we all suck together. It doesn't matter how good the pot roast is; if the rent comes out of their account the wrong way, we all suck together. They won't differentiate *you* from *you*. When they've had a bad service experience, it's a failure for the team as a whole.

"But ... we *succeed* together too. So, why not wear the same uniform? That way, if you walk by a resident—whether you're in nursing or housekeeping—they can say, 'Excuse me, but I have a problem. Can you help me?' You may not be the person who solves their problem, but you now have an opportunity to create a customer service experience. You can listen to their issue and call the appropriate team. And you can thank them for giving you the opportunity to serve them."

That's why everyone at Seasons wears a black golf shirt and a company name tag. That simple practice allows the staff to connect to the residents more often and more easily and to have more meaningful interactions with them.

* * *

Communication happens in a thousand ways, every day. Learn to recognize opportunities to create *connection* through these communications—connection between staff and customers, between management and staff, among your various teams, and among members of the same team.

BUT WAIT—BEFORE YOU GO!

Here are a few more ideas to keep in mind when creating connective communications:

- The best stories are about challenges that are overcome, conflicts that are resolved, problems that are solved. They are mini hero tales.

- Embed your culture in all of your communications, and it will become engrained in your employees and your customers.

CHAPTER FOUR

BE THE CONNECTOR

U ltimately, whether a company develops a connective culture or not comes down to its leadership. One of the most important and profound questions a leader can ask themselves is, "Do I really *want* to be a connector or not?" A single individual with a strong intention of building connectivity can transform an entire organization—and that organization can in turn change the world. That is not an overstatement. You have that capacity as a leader.

The issue of Connecting is especially relevant today, in a way that goes far beyond the workplace. The world we live in has become deeply divided. Groups and ideologies have become entrenched in their thinking and have turned the "other side" into enemies. Almost everywhere you look, globally speaking, you see an us-versus-them mentality. People are seeking security and identity within their own tribes rather than within the greater global community. Whichever side of the political spectrum you stand on, it's impossible to deny that divisiveness characterizes our times.

So the issue of building connections is no trivial matter. It is the defining issue of our era, and the ability to build connections is a leadership skill that is in massive demand, both on the company-level scale and the global one. I'm not saying you will change the world by creating a culture of connectivity in your company, but I'm also not saying you won't.

Connectivity is an area where your leadership can have massive ripple effects. If you actively seek to create richer connections—between workers and management, among your team members, between your company and its customers—your efforts can multiply outward. But in order to get started, you must (as Gandhi famously said) BE the change you want to see in your world. That means you must develop within yourself a connector's mentality.

How? There are certain key traits that connectors possess. I'm not saying that reading about a set of desirable qualities will transform you into a wholly new kind of person and leader, but I am saying this: every *small* change you make in these areas can have immediate and large effects. And as you see these effects take hold, further growth will be stimulated.

Here are some traits I believe connective leaders possess—either naturally or by developing them in themselves …

A "UNITE VERSUS DIVIDE" MENTALITY

Probably the most crucial quality of a connective leader is a genuine desire to unite people rather than divide them. This quality is rarer than it may seem. In my experience, many people pay lip service to the idea of building unity but are dividers or separators at heart. They are quick to point the finger at others, accusing *them* of being dividers, while doing little to build common ground themselves.

To bring people together, you must care about relationships. Connection can't be accomplished by policies, procedures, and practices. Unless your true intent, as a leader, is to find common ground between individuals and groups, any attempt to create unity will be doomed to failure.

I was reminded of this in forceful fashion when I went to work for a large company some years back. My first day on the job, I was given a huge contract to read as part of my orientation. This contract had

Probably the most crucial quality of a connective leader is a genuine desire to unite people rather than divide them.

been written up by a large, well-known accounting and consulting firm. The contract essentially spelled out how the operations team and the sales/marketing team were supposed to work together. Yes, the leadership team had actually paid a consultant a hefty six-figure sum to write a *contract* on how two key components of the company were going to work together—thinking that a contract would somehow do the job of making things work.

On day one, it became clear to me that there was absolutely no *relationship* between operations (my department) and sales/marketing and that this was a major obstacle slowing down our success. You see, in my view, everyone in a company works in sales—from housekeeping to general management. Why? Because we're all delivering on the promise our sales and marketing team is selling. And if everyone doesn't have a thorough understanding of that promise, there is no way they can be doing their jobs effectively.

I knew that if my ops team was not delivering on the promise the sales/marketing team was selling, then we were not delivering on the brand. We were not providing the service experience our customers were paying for and expecting.

And yet, no attempt had been made to bring the ops and sales teams together. Instead, management had created this 150-page legalese contract that was somehow supposed to make a relationship magically happen.

Here's the thing about contracts: you don't enter into contracts to make relationships work. You enter into contracts in case you need to *break* relationships. Contracts give you your exit clause. Sure, they spell out what everyone is supposed to be doing and what execution should look like all around, but the only time you pull the contract out of your drawer is when you decide, "The other guys are not doing what I want. How do I get out of this?"

A contract does not help two parties work together; it simply provides the rules of engagement. Previous to my arrival, leadership's attitude had basically been, "Here are the rules of engagement. You guys fight it out, and whoever wins, that's what we'll do." Ouch.

The ingredient that makes two sides work together is *relationship*, and that was what was absent here. I genuinely wanted that to change. So the first thing I did was reach out to the sales/marketing team—by showing an interest in what they were doing—and start to build a relationship with them. Once I had developed some trust with the sales and marketing people, I went to work on creating relationships between the whole ops team and the sales and marketing people and establishing robust communications back and forth. Before long, the ops team understood what our customers' expectations were, which helped to guide them in their day-to-day efforts to create great customer experiences. And they, in turn, were able to help the sales team craft more specific and realistic service promises. A whole new synergy began to build within the company.

The point of this story is not to pat myself on the back but to show that when a leader's true intention is to unite rather than divide, amazing things can happen.

To be a connector, you must be inclusive and accepting of others outside your comfort zone. You must recognize that a diverse team—made up of different strengths, points of view, values, and approaches—is vastly stronger than a homogenous team.

CURIOSITY

All of this starts with curiosity. To be a connector, you must be genuinely interested in people who are not like yourself—their preferences, their values, their cultures, their lifestyles, their concerns, their fears, their motivations. You must be passionate about a broad spectrum of humanity. You must believe that a diversity of background, talent, opinion, and approach makes for a stronger team than a roomful of people who all have the same characteristics and talents. Imagine a football team where everyone was a three-hundred-pound offensive lineman.

In these tribal times, we tend to build bonds with people who think as we do while excluding those who look and think differently. But a company must be able to serve a wide range of customers. That means its internal team must also be made up of a wide range of people—who are able to work together for a common vision.

Building connections between people with a wide spectrum of backgrounds, cultures, and talents is not easy. It must start with a heartfelt desire on the part of the leader to *know*, rather than exclude, the "other." Tolerance is not enough. Rather, the attitude should be, "I LOVE the fact that you are different from me, and I am hungry to understand your perspective." Only if the leader exhibits this attitude will it spread to other people in the organization.

Curiosity extends beyond an interest in people. You must also be curious about fields of knowledge outside your own. You must have a real interest in the work that every single department in your company does. Only then will you be able to meaningfully connect the data points you receive from all over the company. Only then will you be able to find innovative ways to bring all of your departments together toward common goals.

Your curiosity should reach outside your industry, as well. The next great idea could be out there, in a business very different from your own. Perhaps, for example, there is something about the way McDonald's sets up its workstations that could inspire you as an auto parts manufacturer. In our case, looking to Disney, an entertainment company, provided the blueprint for the kind of customer service experience we wanted to create.

HUMILITY

Of course, in order to benefit from curiosity, you must be open to new ideas. Humility is a quality that goes hand in hand with curiosity. You must be accepting of the fact that you don't know everything and be willing to absorb, and build on, the knowledge of others.

Humble leaders do not surround themselves with yes-men; rather, they surround themselves with people who are smarter and more talented than they are. The members of your management team should represent a wide range of talents and expertise that you yourself do not possess. A humble leader is not threatened by the expertise of others but rather is *energized* by it. It is this love of others' talent that builds great connections with great people.

Many people confuse humility with weakness or lowliness. Nothing could be further from the truth. A humble person possesses tremendous power and strength, a quiet sense of security that does not require propping up from others. He or she does not feel diminished by the strength of others but rather *added to*. An ego-driven leader, on the other hand, loves the trappings of power and seeks to wield dominion over others.

Humble leaders draw talented people to their teams because they work to empower others, not dominate them. They are able to encourage and celebrate the growth of their team members. They are driven to both acquire and impart knowledge; they seek mentoring for themselves while offering mentoring to others. They strive to develop new leaders within the company so that the company can function and thrive in their own absence.

> The measure of a truly great leader is that the company is able to continue to thrive in their absence.

I am sometimes concerned when I see a company that depends on a highly identifiable and charismatic leader, such as a Richard Branson or a Steve Jobs. I worry that the company will flounder in the absence of such a leader. Sometimes the truest and best leaders are those who unselfishly work toward training new leadership and creating great succession plans within their companies. In fact, the measure of a truly great leader is that the company is able to continue to thrive in their absence.

Humble leaders support their employees' growth, even when a team member outgrows the company. A leader in our company, for example, recently had this conversation with a young manager: "I can see your aspirations are more ambitious than what we may be able to offer you at this time. If you're not happy developing at the pace we're moving and you need to look elsewhere for opportunities, I completely understand. So let's do this: we'll continue to work together on your career path at the best pace that we can. But if you need to go someplace new, let us help you find the best place for you. Because someday you may want to come back here. And with the skills you gain elsewhere, you're going to have value to us because you already understand our culture, plus you'll have that new skill set. And we love you. So I won't feel bad if you leave; in fact, I'll feel happy both for you and for us."

TRUST

To have that kind of conversation with a team member, there must be a foundation of trust. Your people must believe you have their best interests at heart—otherwise they will not be honest and open with you about their career intentions. The only way they *develop* that belief is by your consistently showing them you are worthy of their highest trust.

That means you never take advantage of them or use what they tell you in confidence as a weapon against them. You never take credit for their ideas but always bend over backward to make sure they are acknowledged. You don't lie to them. In fact, you don't lie at all. You are accountable for every decision you make—the popular ones and the unpopular ones.

In order for your team members to trust you, you must be a person of character and integrity. You must honor your word and have principles and values that guide you.

Nothing builds connection in a team better than trust; nothing ruptures connection like broken trust. Trust is the heart and soul of a Connected organization. And it starts with the company's leadership.

LIKABILITY

In addition to trustworthiness, connective leaders have engaging personalities that make people want to come together around them. They have a "likability" factor—some combination of empathy, warmth, accessibility, sense of humor, and perhaps a mystery ingredient or two. Likability is a hard attribute to define, but at minimum, a leader should not be a seven-letter word starting with *A*.

It is hard to know if you are likable; that's entirely for others to decide. Sometimes asking for feedback from people you trust can help you understand your likability factor and "repair" areas where people may find you off-putting.

When I began at Seasons, I had just moved on from a big public company. I'd felt it was important, in that previous role, to represent myself as a corporate professional, an identifiable problem solver for the company. So I'd always show up in a suit. I continued this practice at Seasons, at first, when I would visit our properties. It wasn't long before one of the general managers took me aside and said to me, "Mike, you know, when you show up in the blue suit, people think you're unapproachable. They don't necessarily think you're a friendly or likable person. They're not seeing the real you. I would suggest that when you come to the properties, you go out of your way to connect with people in a more informal way."

Needless to say, I haven't worn a tie in years.

It is extraordinarily difficult for people to come together and go the extra mile for someone they don't like. So if there is anything within your control that's getting in the way of your likability factor, it's wise (if a bit painful) to find out about it and take steps to correct it.

COURAGEOUS STANDARD-BEARING

Many middle managers, however, in an attempt to be likable and build connections with their team members, resort to a very destructive habit: distancing themselves from company decisions they feel may be unpopular. They'll say things like, "This policy is from corporate; I don't agree with it, but I have to enforce it," or "My hands are tied. My bosses want to do it this way, even though I think it's dumb."

Although this kind of tactic can seemingly make a manager more likable to his direct reports, it ultimately undermines a company's culture. It creates an "us and them" mentality between the frontline workers and "corporate." It suggests there is a schism between the company's upper and middle management and that the company is divided in its values. Employees can only be fully connected to an organization that is unified and connected within itself.

That is why it is essential that connective leaders serve as courageous standard-bearers for the company. Although it is fine—in fact, it is healthy and essential—to voice opposition to a policy you disagree with *while that policy is being formulated*, you must get fully on board with it once it has been agreed on by the top executive team. Whether you endorse the policy in every last detail or not, you must speak for it as if it comes directly from you. You must be accountable to it, not undermine it.

Courageous standard-bearing throughout a company's management team shows unity and connectivity within the organization. There are no "camps" or "sides" in such a scenario. There is one culture only. Employees can connect to this kind of culture in an unconflicted way.

If you seriously disagree with an existing policy—for example, if it raises ethical issues for you—it is your responsibility to address this issue with your bosses. Make a strong case as to why you believe a different approach would be better. If the policy stands regardless, you then have a decision to make. Will you stay with the company or not? If you decide to stay, that means you have decided to fully support the company's policies and practices.

EMOTIONAL COOLNESS AND MATURITY

One final aspect of connective leadership worthy of mention here is emotional maturity. It is important that your team understands that you are a person who will respond to challenges in a cool, calm, and thoughtful manner and that you will not allow your emotions to make decisions for you. People only feel comfortable confiding in a leader they trust will not react in anger, defensiveness, or hurt feelings when difficult issues are raised. No one wants to be yelled at or blamed or made to feel they've caused another person pain.

Being emotionally mature does not mean you are emotionless; it means you can be counted on to *manage* your emotions so the best possible decision can be made.

I had an experience not long ago that underscores the importance of emotional coolness and also illustrates many of the other ideas we've been talking about in this chapter.

I chair the board of the Ontario Retirement Communities Association, and we do a joint venture annually with an association of long-term-care providers; it's a big conference we put on together. Well, the CEOs of these two associations didn't have great chemistry. One was very brash and unreceptive; the other was a bit more on the indignant side. They couldn't seem to connect, mainly due to their emotional orientations. So, the joint venture agreement was coming due for renewal, and it specified things like how we would pay for expenses and how we would share revenue. The agreement had first been signed about twenty years earlier, at a time when the retirement business represented only a small portion of the overall attendance.

And so it had made sense, at that time, for there to be an 80/20–type revenue share. But now attendance was almost 50/50 between the two associations, and a squaring up was needed.

During the negotiations it became clear to me that there was a lot of emotion in both sides' anchored positions. And neither was willing to budge. There were heated discussions about dissolving our union. I took it upon myself to have a side conversation with my counterpart, the board chair of the other association. I said, "John, there is zero chance that our current approach is going to yield productive results. There's also zero rationale for us to compete with each other and not share in the joint resources of this great event. So let's just agree that we're better together than apart. Is that a fair statement?" He said it was.

"What we need to recognize," I continued, "is that our two CEOs are emotionally anchored to their positions and that they must reframe them. Your CEO has a sense of historical entitlement and sees us as the poor stepchild who should be happy to receive whatever breadcrumbs fall from the table. But reality has changed. So reframing our relationship is critical, and that needs to be a tough conversation you have with your CEO.

"I need to do the same with my CEO," I continued, "because her petulant, indignant position is not going to yield any benefits. At the end of the day, both sides have anchors that need to be lifted so we can end up somewhere that's a little bit fairer. Neither side is going to get what it *wants*, but we have to decide what we *need* in order to move the joint venture agreement forward."

He said, "You're right. Thank you for your leadership on this. I will have that tough conversation." He did, and so did I.

This led to fourteen months of earnest, open, and honest negotiations that resulted in an agreement that everyone felt was very fair. We didn't have to involve any lawyers; we didn't have to do any forensic accounting. And we ended up with a playing field that was far more level. The process even led to some leadership changes that were healthy for both organizations. What brought about the whole change was a dash of emotional maturity and coolness on both sides. And—most of all—a genuine desire to unite instead of divide.

* * *

Business is a human enterprise. Connecting human beings to one another is the key to every single thing of value that happens in business. Your biggest decision as a business leader is, *Are you going to be a connector or not?*

BUT WAIT—BEFORE YOU GO!

Here are a few additional things you can do to become a great Connector:

- Be decisive—After you've reached out to everyone on your team and collected their input, synthesize that input and make a firm decision. Move from ambiguity to clarity. Clarity is what connects a team together toward common goals.

- Be accountable—A connective leader never passes the buck or blames others for decisions that don't work out. Accountability from the top creates trust and safety within teams.

- Celebrate—Go out of your way to celebrate your team members' successes. Be a relentless cheerleader. Constantly accentuate the positive in your employees and downplay the negative. Lift people up—don't put them down.

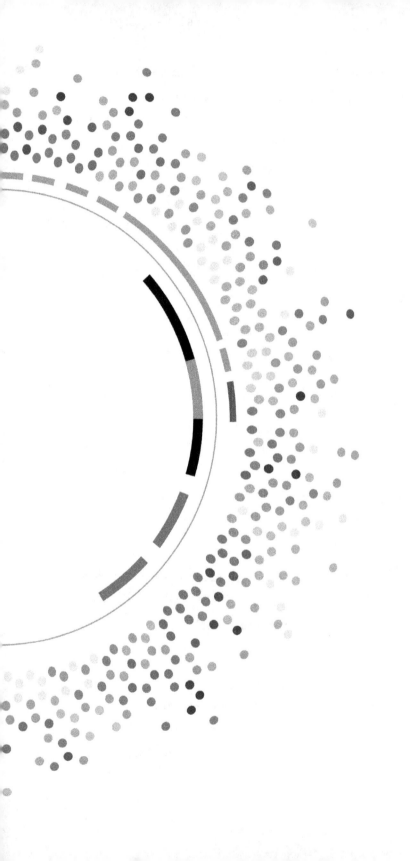

PART II:
CARING

Now let's move on to the second, and most important, of the Three Cs: Caring.

Caring is the chief value-add ingredient we offer at Seasons. It is our "special sauce." And yet, caring is the one thing that can't be taught or forced. You can't MAKE employees care.

You can hire staff based on their propensity *to care, but unless you* inspire *staff to care for the things that you value by creating a consistent culture of caring, you will not be able to sustain caring on a day-to-day basis.*

So how does an organization create a culture that inspires employees to care, and what are the things that you want them to care about?

It all starts with your business vision. You must understand why you are in your chosen business and how you create value. Thus far in this book, we have been talking about the "softer" aspects of running a human enterprise, but I want you to know that there are sound business principles behind our Connect, Care, Change model. Toward that end, we use a conceptual tool that many other businesses use to help them understand the value they are creating: Porter's Value Chain. This tool was originally designed for product-intensive businesses such as manufacturing, but, with some adjustments, it can be useful in service-intensive businesses as well.

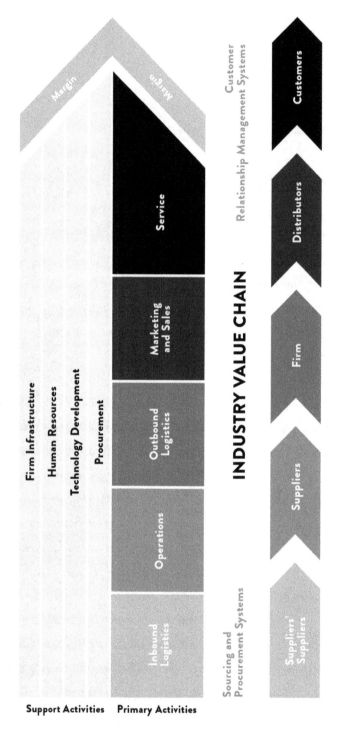

TRADITIONAL PORTER'S VALUE CHAIN

Margin

Margin

Support Activities

Firm Infrastructure

Human Resources

Technology Development

Procurement

Primary Activities

Inbound Logistics

Operations

Outbound Logistics

Marketing and Sales

Service

INDUSTRY VALUE CHAIN

Sourcing and Procurement Systems

Customer Relationship Management Systems

Suppliers' Suppliers

Suppliers

Firm

Distributors

Customers

With that in mind, I have distilled Porter's Value Chain to this simplified model that worked for us:

SEASONS VALUE CHAIN

Let's break it down:

LEADERSHIP EXCELLENCE: *This is demonstrated when an organization is able to clearly articulate its vision, mission, and commonly shared purpose (caring), and when its leaders are able to communicate, through their actions and words, what is valued and what will be measured.*

+

STAFF EXCELLENCE: *This is demonstrated when staff is recruited and trained in order to be able to execute on plans and behaviors that will fulfill the commonly shared purpose (caring).*

+

CUSTOMER EXPERIENCES: *This is demonstrated when staff is given the tools and freedom to execute on the commonly shared purpose (caring) and create valued customer experiences for which customers willingly pay.*

=

RESULTS/PROFITS/SUCCESS.

We don't necessarily show this formula to staff when we are hiring, training, and supporting them, but it sits in the background of everything we do.

The "commonly shared purpose" on which we execute, in our case, is caring. Caring is the differentiator by which we create our value as a company. Everything we do as a company is designed to support caring.

Given that caring can't be forced, how do we make it happen?

In order to answer that question, we're going to look at the three main elements of our value chain over the next three chapters. And I'd like to begin with the element that is most easy to observe and understand at ground level: customer experience.

Caring is delivered, on a day-to-day basis, through the great customer service experiences we strive to create.

CHAPTER FIVE

THE CUSTOMER EXPERIENCE

SAM FLIES AGAIN

Sam was a ninety-three-year-old resident of one of our communities, a veteran of WWII. Sam was a bit of a crusty guy, his face set into a permafrown—not the easiest person to approach if you didn't know him. Beneath his prickly exterior, though, Sam was a gentleman and a colorful character.

Sam didn't talk a lot about himself. That was why Jake, one of our activity staffers, was surprised one day when he overheard Sam telling a long and animated story to one of the other residents. From what Jake could piece together, the story Sam was telling was about the "big war." Evidently, Sam had been a paratrooper and had been part of a key battle.

In the days following his storytelling, Sam seemed unusually quiet and thoughtful. More than once, Jake spotted him staring wistfully out the window—not sadly so much as "lost in thought."

Jake's instinct was that the story Sam had told had stirred something up in him.

"Hey, Sam," said Jake one morning when Sam was drinking his coffee in the bistro. "You mind if I join you?"

"Be my guest," said Sam with his crafty smile.

Jake sat with his coffee and said, "I couldn't help overhearing you the other day, when you were talking to Marty. I didn't know you had jumped out of planes in World War II. I'd love to hear your story if you don't mind telling it again."

Sam proceeded to tell Jake about how he had played a role in the invasion at Normandy on D-Day, which led to the liberation of France. Sam was part of a battalion of Canadian paratroopers that had landed behind enemy lines and worked its way toward the beach, cornering the German troops as the Allied forces arrived by sea.

Prior to the battle, Sam had parachuted from a plane, along with thousands of others, in the dead of night.

"I still remember that drop like it was yesterday," Sam told Jake. "Falling through the sky in that pitch-black night, the cold wind whipping my face, all my brothers-in-arms around me. Part of me was terrified, but the experience was the most alive I've ever felt. I miss that feeling."

At that moment, Jake got an idea. He didn't say anything to Sam, though. He needed to do some research first.

A couple of days later, Jake spotted Sam in the garden and said, "Sam, got a minute? I want to share a crazy idea with you. I'm not telling you to try it; I'm just giving you some information. I found a place not too far away from here that offers tandem skydiving jumps. They give you some training in the morning, then you do your jump, with an instructor, that same afternoon. They have a perfect safety record, and they jump with people of all ages."

"I'm in," said Sam, without blinking an eye.

And so Jake set up the jump and volunteered to provide Sam's transportation. And a few weeks later, on a cool day in October, Sam found himself plummeting through the sky near London, Ontario, strapped to a parachuting instructor, having a peak experience at age ninety-three.

After the event, Sam walked to Jake's car with a twinkle in his eye and a spring in his step.

I didn't learn about Sam's jump until after it had happened, but when I did, I called him on the phone. "You've got to tell me, Sam," I said, "what possessed you to jump out of a plane."

He replied, "Mike, I'm ninety-three. If I didn't do it now, I don't know when I might have had another chance. It was such a thrill. It made me relive that moment when I felt such incredible pride and such fear and aliveness as well. But more than that, it gave me a chance to do something for all my friends I lost in that battle. I jumped to commemorate them as well."

I felt myself choking up, but still, I was curious to know: "What did your family think when you told them about your plans to jump?"

"My daughter thought I was crazy and pretty much forbade me from doing it."

"Well, good for you for standing up to her," I said.

"Stand up to her?" he replied. "I'm not *that* crazy. I just said, 'Okay, you're right, dear ...'" Then, with a badass little growl in his voice, he added, "And then I went and did it anyway."

How do you think Sam rated that experience as a customer?

CUSTOMER SERVICE IS EVERYTHING

Great customer experiences are a result of great customer service. That means something different in every industry, but in each case it comes down to delivering on, and/or exceeding, the promise you make to your customer.

In this chapter, we're going to look at how we do that at Seasons. The specifics might not be the same in your industry, but still, understanding the type of thinking that goes into delivering on *our* promises might give you some inspiration of your own, whether you own a pizza restaurant, a dentistry practice, or an interior design service. It's the *thought process* behind delivering great customer service that is more important than the specific details.

What is our promise at Seasons? Essentially this: "In addition to providing all the basic services we contract for (housing, meals, medical support, activities, etc.), we are committed to creating meaningful moments where you feel like this is your home."

To deliver on our promise becomes a two-tiered endeavor. First, we must satisfy our residents' base-level requirements on a strictly *transactional* level. That is, we must provide all the concrete services we specify in our contract: a certain number of meals per day or month, housekeeping, laundry services, pills delivered on time, and so on—and at a high-quality level.

But above the compliance-level stuff is what I call the *nontransactional* level. These are interactions that do not have a concrete dollar value; they are unrelated to the residents' cost-based expectations (i.e., "If I pay x, I should get y"). They are relationship based. A great customer service experience at Seasons looks exactly like an interaction between two human beings if there was no money involved. Genuine caring is involved.

BRILLIANT AT THE BASICS

Here's a simple example. Let's say you know that every day when Mrs. Smith comes down for breakfast, she likes to have black coffee, piping hot, the minute she sits down. So you show up with her hot coffee without her having to ask. This shows her that you've made the effort to note her preferences and that you are connected to the way she lives her daily life.

Next, you might consider some of her food preferences. "Hey, Mrs. Smith, I was just looking at the menu. You know what's for lunch today? Your favorite—chicken pie." So now you're creating a sense of anticipation for what's going to happen later on. Again, simple. But meaningful.

Now ... after breakfast maybe Mrs. Smith goes to the fitness room where she does her daily exercise routine. The instructor knows Mrs. Smith is interested in fitness, so she says, "Mrs. Smith, you're going to love today, because we're going to put you through your paces and add a little something new to your routine." And so you're creating a bit of excitement. You're also telling Mrs. Smith you care about her health and support her fitness goals.

And so on, throughout the day.

None of these are *wow* moments. They're about being brilliant at the basics—knowing your customers, connecting with them, caring about the things that are important to them, and making an effort to produce experiences they value so they can have a great day. Imagine if you, as a customer, went through an entire day where every interaction was thoughtfully customized in this way. At the end of the day, you'd be feeling like, "Wow, I should never have lived anywhere else. And I never will again. I want to tell all my friends to move in here."

Now let's say Mrs. Smith comes down for breakfast and she's *not* having a great start to her day. Maybe she just found out her daughter can't come to visit this weekend because she's just been diagnosed with something or her kids are sick. So Mrs. Smith is dealing with disappointment and worry. As soon as she shows up in the dining room, a staff member might say, "Gee, Mrs. Smith, you don't look so chipper today. Is everything okay?" Mrs. Smith will probably share her concerns, because this staff person has built a relationship with her.

Now the staff has the opportunity to show empathy. "Oh gosh, I'm so sorry, Mrs. Smith; I know you were looking forward to this weekend. Hey, it's not much, but can I get you a slice of that coffee cake you love from my 'private stash'?"

This is not to suggest that a piece of cake can solve all concerns. The specific act of caring we offer is not important; the important thing is that Mrs. Smith *knows we are aware that things aren't great for her and that we care.*

There is no set formula for being brilliant at the basics. Every resident is different, as is every staff person. It's up to us to respond in a personal, spontaneous way to whatever situation we're given.

EASY AND NATURAL

Customer service, when it's really, really good, should look easy. One thing we always tell our staff is that we don't want them to work hard; we want them to work smart. Because when they work smart—that is, pay attention to people and respond honestly to them—it doesn't look hard. It looks like an extension of their own personality.

Here is a simple illustration from a retail setting. The other day, I was grocery shopping, and I stopped in at two stores. As I was checking out of Store A, the cashier asked me in a canned voice, "Any plans for the weekend?" It was an awkward question. I knew she wasn't really interested in my weekend plans. And I knew she'd been trained to ask the question—I'd heard her ask the same thing of the previous customer. The whole thing felt so staged; there was no comfortable way to answer her. I couldn't wait to get out of the store.

As I was checking out of Store B, the cashier commented on a detail on the shirt I was wearing. It sparked him to tell a little story about a recent trip he'd made to a local museum, and then we started chatting about museums in the area. Two nearby cashiers got involved in the conversation, adding their personal commentary. We were all laughing and joking. As I exited the store, I felt I'd had a real exchange with some real human beings—and as a bonus, I'd also learned of a museum I wanted to check out. I walked back to my car feeling bright and alive.

The difference? Store A had created a "forced" customer experience, which was uncomfortable for everyone. Store B had empowered its employees to respond spontaneously to customers and to be themselves. Which store do you suppose I want to return to?

LIKE HOME

When you move in to a Seasons community, we commit ourselves to creating meaningful moments where you will feel like it's home. We may not be able to make your six-hundred-square-foot apartment *look* like home—especially if you've lived in a four-bedroom family house for the last forty years—but our goal is to make our places *feel* like home regardless.

Home is a feeling, not a place. What is the feeling of home? It is a feeling of "I belong here. This is the place where I can relax and be myself. This is the place where I'm surrounded by people who know me, welcome me, care about me, and care *for* me."

It's the personal, caring moments, more than anything else, that create the feeling of home. Here's a simple example I observed in a recent visit to one of our sites. Mary, a resident, had an adult daughter who typically took her to her doctor's appointments. This particular week, the daughter was away and had forgotten to tell us. So when

Mary came to us worriedly and said, "I have an appointment, and my daughter's not here," the manager thought for a moment and said, "You know what? It's my lunchtime. Why don't we go together in my car? It'll give us a chance to chat and catch up."

Again, a small thing. But huge in its own way and personal. Legally, I would prefer if our employees didn't take residents out in their own personal vehicles, but you can't deny that it was heartfelt and generous.

UNDERSTAND YOUR CUSTOMER

In order to provide great customer care in a way that feels meaningful to your particular customers, you must make a genuine effort to understand who your customers are and what is important to them.

In order to provide great customer care in a way that feels meaningful to your particular customers, you must make a genuine effort to understand who your customers are and what is important to them. Your customer base has distinctive needs, life issues, and preferences. The better you can understand what these issues are, the better care you can provide.

LOSS AND FEAR

For our customers, for example, the decision to move into a community like ours, one that offers assisted services, often comes on the heels of a major loss of some kind. So *loss* is a prominent issue for most of our folks.

Loss of independence is one type of loss. There is a very high correlation, for instance, between losing a driver's license and moving into a retirement community.

There is also a high correlation between loss of a spouse and moving into a retirement home. Loss of mobility is also extremely common—perhaps the person has suffered a hip fracture as a result of a fall and now can no longer manage stairs. Loss of health is common, as is loss of identity; many of our new customers have recently become widows/widowers or retired from lifelong careers.

Grief and sadness typically accompany loss. This is why our staff is trained in dealing with such things. We try to understand the particular loss each resident has suffered and to deal with that loss with sensitivity and care. We also try to offer positive new options—such as social and community activities—that can help offset the grief and to accentuate the *gains* that come along with moving to a retirement community.

Fear is another major issue for seniors in transition. Our new residents are often fearful about starting a new lifestyle and fitting in with a new community. They are fearful about end-of-life issues and about being perceived as "elderly." They may not *want* to fit into their new community because they perceive the others as "old" and still see themselves as young. The default response to most of these fears is just to stay home and hide out. So we train our staff to gently address these fears as they work toward helping residents maximize their new options and come out of their suites. We also try to deputize some "service ambassadors" from among our high-functioning residents. They can help new folks get past their fears.

PURPOSE

Purpose is another huge issue for retirement community customers. People who have a meaningful reason to get out of bed every morning are healthier, happier, and live longer. They don't feel like a burden to others; rather, they feel like an asset, and they want to contribute.

Without that sense of purpose, it is easy for our population to feel as if they're in the "dying" chapter of their lives. So we focus on purpose and self-actualization quite a lot.

For example, we have a program we call Seniorocity. This is an outreach program where we help residents continue to do meaningful work in the community through various organizations and activities like the Rotarians or Kiwanis Club.

We also have a great many fitness-oriented events and contests. Folks can compete within the home and/or against other homes. Often these events are connected to events that are happening in the world, like the Olympics or the Pan American Games.

Some residents may want to be part of the quilting club. Others may want to share their special recipes, so we bring them in on the food council. This is a great opportunity for us to connect with people who have spent their lives cooking for their families but now feel removed from that important purpose. We have a strategic relationship with the Food Network and with celebrity chefs like Anna and Michael Olson. Once per quarter they go into one of our communities and cook a signature dish with a live audience. They get to meet our residents, and we livestream the whole thing online. These are popular events.

We have some communities that make wine. The result is not always a prize-winning vintage, but that's irrelevant. These folks make wine because it's fun to make and drink. We also have a couple of communities that make beer for their own consumption too. Happy hour on Fridays!

We have woodshops where residents can bring all their tools from their former home and set up in a space in the building. On our campus in St. Thomas—that's the railway capital of Canada—we have a hobby room where residents can build miniature railways.

We're constantly looking for new activities and options that allow residents to pursue a sense of purpose.

CULTURE, GEOGRAPHY, BACKGROUND

Another way we work hard to understand our clientele is by being aware of, and sensitive to, geographical/cultural issues and other "demographically driven" preferences.

There's nothing like a farming community, for example, to tell you how crappy your food is—if you're cooking the way they eat in the city. So in a farming community like Strathroy, Ontario, where many of our people are Dutch Mennonites, we don't put rice or pasta on the menu too often. It's meat and potatoes. You have to understand that. You also have to provide access to spiritual, religious, and community services/resources that are meaningful and important to these folks.

Amherstburg, Ontario, is an example of a community that is less rural. It also happens to have a large Italian population. So here we need to have *more* pasta on the menu; in fact, we always offer a pasta dish as an alternative to the main special.

Food is just one way we adapt to our clients' general tastes and backgrounds; we also do it through the activities we offer, the resources we provide, the clubs we create, the trips we organize, and the values and needs we strive to accommodate.

I am often surprised by how many opportunities for great customer service are missed by businesses that don't make the effort to understand who their customers are. These businesses take a vendor-centric approach: here are the products and services *we* offer—take them or leave them. But when you make the effort to understand the particular population you serve—whether that's busy commuters, teenagers, rural homeowners, or new moms—you open up a whole new dimension of customer service opportunities: What problems do my customers have that I can solve? What are some ways I can make their lives easier? What strategic partnerships might I enter to increase the value I'm offering?

Bottom line: if you don't understand the human beings you are serving, perhaps you should not be in the customer service business.

MEASURING CARE

Every business must have ways of measuring the value it is attempting to provide. Is that value really being provided in the way you intend? Are your customers responding favorably to it? Is it creating profit?

In our business at Seasons, it can be tricky to quantify the value we provide, because our "special sauce" consists of caring moments. And, as I noted earlier, these moments are nontransactional in nature. They don't translate into a concrete dollar value. Still, some form of measuring must occur so we can know whether we're creating the kind of customer experience we strive to create. Here are some of the indirect ways we measure the care we provide:

- Spending patterns. As in most businesses, our customers can vote with their wallets. They can move out if they're not happy with the services we are providing. Of course, changes in spending are not as fluid in our industry as they are in, say, the retail business—people don't move out of residences impulsively or for casual reasons—but still, whenever we see a trend of increasing vacancies, we know there are issues that need addressing.

- Referrals. In a related way, an *increase* in referrals is a positive sign. Our aim is for our residents to love living at Seasons so much that they tell all their friends to move in. In an ideal scenario, customers make referrals spontaneously because they're so happy living with us. But we also offer incentives for residents to make referrals. Whenever we notice an increasing need to offer incentives, that means people are not making referrals spontaneously. We try to find out why.

- Complaints. At Seasons, we ask for feedback a lot, and we make it easy for customers to complain. One simple way we track customer satisfaction is to note an increase or decrease in customer complaints. It is impossible to run a 100 percent complaint-free business, of course, so we "expect" a small base number of complaints per month. The vast majority of these are resolved quickly and directly. But whenever we notice a steady increase in complaints—or a rise in the *escalation* of complaints to higher management levels—we know something is off.

- In our business, complaints cannot always be taken at face value. A certain percentage of our senior population views complaining as an art form. But also, a complaint may mask another issue. Recently, for example, I was sitting in a board meeting with one of our investment partners. He leaned to me and said, "Hey, Mike, I just got a text from a guy we're doing a pitch to. His mom lives at Seasons, and she just told him the food at her place has 'gone to hell in a handbasket.' What do I say to him?"

- Right then and there, I texted the manager of that Seasons site and gave her the woman's name. The manager promptly texted back, "Actually, as recently as yesterday, that resident said she was very happy with the food. Her weight is being

93

maintained, she's enjoying the company in the dining room, and she's enjoying the service. She did mention to me yesterday, however, that her son hasn't been to see her in a month."

- I laughed to myself, turned to the board member, and said, "That resident doesn't have an issue with the food. She's complaining so her son will engage with her and come visit. She misses him. Tell him to call her more often."

- Error rates. In addition to tracking complaints, we track error rates as well. If we notice an increase in medication errors, food service errors, billing errors, and so on, we know this indicates a drop in our level of staff engagement. That means care is suffering too.

- Resident council. Another way in which we solicit feedback and take a general "temperature reading" of our residents is the resident council. Participating in the council includes monthly meetings where we talk about issues the residents ask us to address and report on where we are in our course of action. We also invite people to bring up new concerns or needs they might have with any of the departments.

- To show that we take all feedback seriously, we work hard to ensure that past complaints are dealt with in demonstrable ways. The manager conducting the council meeting might say, for instance, "We read the suggestion box and saw that on November 12 a lot of folks complained about the pork chops. The chef is here, and he's going to talk about that."

- Then the chef might address the group and say, "We tried a new cut of pork, but our recipe was wrong. I'm so sorry about that. I'm open to suggestions about a better recipe we might try." We take transparent accountability for what went right and what went wrong.

- It's important to have a live forum with your customers, because this gives you a much more accurate reading of their attitudes than you can get from a paper survey. Attendance levels at these meetings is another key indicator. If attendance is slipping or if only the same ten or twelve people show up every time, we know we're about to receive a complaint letter.

- Surveys. We do paper satisfaction surveys too, on a regular basis. Some people are more comfortable reporting dissatisfaction on an anonymous form than in person. We pay particular attention to *patterns* of response. If we suddenly get an increase in poor ratings for housekeeping, for example, we know there's an issue with that department.

Here again, engagement is a key factor. If only 20 or 30 percent of residents are bothering to fill out their surveys, that's a red flag too.

- Engagement. Engagement in general is a meaningful marker to watch. An engaged customer is a happy customer. If we notice participation levels going down in any area—activities, fitness room usage, meals, social events—we know disengagement is occurring. And that is something we need to address.

- Letters. Perhaps the most powerful way we receive indications of satisfaction or dissatisfaction is through spontaneously written letters. People don't write letters casually; they do so only when seriously motivated. So when I receive a letter of complaint from a customer or family member, I know this is a matter I need to look into personally and with some urgency.

- On the flip side, after a loved one passes away, I often receive "love letters" from family members. Here's an excerpt from one such letter: "Mom truly enjoyed her best life when living with you. She spoke so highly of everyone who took care of her. We are immensely grateful she spent her last years there; they were the most valuable time we had with her."

- A letter like that is pure gold, and I instantly want to share it with the whole team. It is the best possible testimony that our staff people are providing the one thing we can't force them to provide: caring.

- From the heart.

BUT WAIT—BEFORE YOU GO!

Here are a few more ideas to keep in mind when thinking about the customer experience:

- *Relational* moments ultimately contribute FAR more to the bottom line than transactional moments—even though their effect can't be measured.

- When great customer service is occurring, everyone looks like they're enjoying themselves—because they are!

- When you build relationships with customers through caring, meaningful moments, they are MUCH more forgiving of you when you mess up.

CHAPTER SIX

STAFF EXCELLENCE

'll repeat it again here: the main value we provide is caring—a nontransactional, relationship-based "add-on" that goes beyond all the contracted services residents sign up for when they join Seasons. Our success in creating caring moments depends entirely on the staff we retain. It is the quality of our staff that differentiates our company from other companies providing similar services. That is why staff excellence is the central link in our value chain.

Staff excellence is a value we take deeply to heart—our entire brand rides on it. Not surprisingly, caring is also at the heart of how we create staff excellence. Caring comes into play in two main ways when we hire and develop staff. First and foremost, we strive to ensure that our staff is focused on caring for customers above all else. Second, we focus on caring for, and about, our staff and encouraging them to care for each other.

It all starts with the hiring process.

HIRING

Caring is an elusive quality. It can't be forced or artificially created. So we need to do everything possible to hire people who possess the caring quality and then to train and support them in expressing it in natural ways. People don't get rich working in our business, so we look for the kind of people who get a natural reward from caring and connecting and who are good at it.

Hiring is a process we think about a lot and take very seriously. That's why, at Seasons, we have developed a hiring process that is rather unique within our industry. Here again, we took our initial inspiration from Disney and then adapted the process for our own purposes.

THE "MEET AND GREET"

Unlike most companies, we don't start our hiring process by poring over résumés and scheduling rounds of interviews. In fact, we don't do any one-on-ones until *after* we've identified a candidate we want to go forward with. So how do we find our people?

Our first step in the hiring process is a "meet and greet." Essentially, we invite in a group of people, twelve to fifteen or so, who have expressed an interest in working with us. These are a mix of frontline applicants and management candidates; we don't differentiate at this stage.

We start by telling them the Seasons story—what we're about, our values, what we expect from employees, what working in our environment is like. We go out of our way to make clear what's negotiable and nonnegotiable and to express our passion for what we do. Our main message is, "This is who we are, and this is what you're walking into. Don't think you're going to change us or skate around our values. It's okay if you decide we're not for you."

There are three main reasons we start with a meet and greet. First, efficiency. We prefer to tell our story once (instead of fifteen times), tell it fully, and tell it well. Second, it helps us whittle down the candidate pool. After people hear what we're up to, a fair number of them say, "These people sound nuts. I'm out." Great, no hard feelings. Finally, it helps us get a good initial read on the people we're interested in pursuing.

To help with the latter, we do group exercises, as part of the meet and greet, that force people to collaborate. You've probably done this type of activity before—simple games like, "You're stranded on a deserted island. Here's a list of twenty items; you can only bring five. Which ones would you bring, and why?" And we break folks up into small teams and watch them work together, focusing on how they collaborate (or not), how they listen (or not), how they respect each other (or not). We notice how easily they laugh, how personable they are.

By observing them working together, we're able to see who is really a "people person," a team player. You can fake that quality in an interview, but it's harder to fake when you're interacting with real people.

We also give people a written exercise during this day-one event, something simple, like, "If you had a superpower, what would it be, and why?" This gives us a chance to assess people's literacy level and their values as well as their creativity, critical thinking, and personality.

Finally, we walk them through our community. We want them to see our staff in action, meet some of our residents, get an actual taste of a Seasons community. And we watch how they react and interact. (There's an added motive in this for us: all of these people, whether we hire them or not, have parents, grandparents, uncles, and aunts they might refer to us based on hearing our presentation and touring our property. We're always doing sales!)

We do all of the above without looking at anyone's résumé. Why? Because we know that individuals don't always live up to their résumés, and vice versa. And interviews aren't always reliable either; a candidate, for example, might be simply having a bad day. That's why we try to gamify the experience a bit—so people don't feel like it's high pressure.

Many people rave about our day-one event, but some complain, "You never gave me an opportunity to showcase my skills and experience." What they don't understand is that they needed to pass our initial hurdle first. We want to know if people appear to be caring individuals and a good fit for us. Only *after* that are we willing to listen to their sales pitch.

Once we've identified some people who are potentially good fits, *that's* when we start to evaluate their résumés. And we try to be open minded and creative in this regard too.

We might say, for example, "This person applied for an opening in dietary, but I see them more as management material." We may not hire them for the job they applied for, but we might call them back three months later and offer them something better.

When and if we do get to the interview process with a candidate, we try to make it an authentic conversation. Sure, we ask some questions about experience and past successes, but mainly we want the candidate to feel they're on an equal plane with us, that they want this job as much as we want them, and that they want it for the right reasons. We try to create a setting where an honest conversation can take place and where we can mutually figure out whether we'd be a fit to work together.

Our goal is to find people who, after the whole interview process, say, "I really wouldn't want to work anywhere else. I'll hold out until you have a position for me here."

ONBOARDING

Once we've chosen a new hire, we customize their onboarding experience based on what they've done and whom we want them to meet. We are very peer-to-peer based when it comes to onboarding. Much of the process involves "shadowing," whereby a new person accompanies an experienced, successful team member and watches how they do things. We try to pair new folks with exemplary individuals who have a good story to tell about the work they do. Our goal is to create a very strong image of what success looks like in each department. For a frontline person, the shadowing usually occurs within their own department. Managers might shadow people from several different departments. During these pairings, we focus on the relational and caring aspects of the job as much as, or more than, the practical details.

With managers, we try to show them what *all-around* excellence looks like to us. We might, for example, take them to the home that has the best kitchen and say, "This dietary team has the highest satisfaction levels among residents and zero turnover. Study this kitchen, and make sure *your* chef is delivering to this standard." The same thing with activities, housekeeping, and so on. "This home rocks. Study what they do."

For the first two weeks of their tenure with us, we don't even allow general managers to set foot in the actual home they will be managing. We don't want anyone telling them, "This is the way we do things here"—because maybe that's the problem. Maybe that's why a change was needed. We don't want the same-old, same-old; we want better.

If a new manager has a gap in their knowledge or experience—for example, in finance—we'll pair them with a general manager who has great strengths in that area. This might go on for the first six months. We try to immerse them in success and excellence. We want everyone we hire to start out with *excellence*, not competence, in mind.

MAINTAINING STAFF EXCELLENCE

Of course, finding and hiring great people is only the start. A lot of effort goes into maintaining and improving staff excellence on an ongoing basis. Here is where having a great culture is so critical. If you have a great culture, new staff will be pulled into it and will become champions of that culture for future staff members. We talk about culture in some other parts of the book, so here we'll look at some other things we do to train, encourage, and support our staff.

RECOGNITION

Positive reinforcement is our prime tool for building excellence. We believe people are much more motivated by recognition and appreciation than by criticism.

Thus, one of the main roles of supervisors and managers is to *catch people doing the right thing.* I encourage managers, if possible, to spend 50 percent of their time out "on the floor" interacting with staff and residents rather than closeted away in their offices. And I urge them, on a daily basis, to pay attention to staff who are exhibiting excellence in any way.

Here's a simple example. The other day I was walking down a hallway, and the housekeeper turned her vacuum cleaner off as I was walking by and said, "Hi, how are you?"

Shutting off the vac was a simple act of courtesy I had never considered before. I asked her if she did this often, and she said, "Yes, each time a resident walks by or a sales tour comes through, I stop the machine and greet people."

I replied, "I think that's part of the reason your occupancy is so good here. Thank you so much for doing that." She smiled in a way that told me my gratitude was meaningful.

One of the "official" ways we recognize staffers for being excellent is our shout-out program. We use our daily team meetings as a great opportunity to say things like, "Hey, a shout-out to Sharon. She got three notes from her team members recognizing her effort in putting together a great activity that went above and beyond what was expected. She did an amazing job."

The shout-out is peer generated; it can also come from a leader catching you doing the right thing. Shout-out suggestions are written on Post-it Notes, and they go into the individual's mailbox. They also go into what we call "the book." At the end of the month, we look at all of the shout-outs in the book, and these often result in service ribbons. I've mentioned these before. The employee gets to wear their service ribbon for the remainder of the calendar year. On January 1, all of the service ribbons come off, and folks need to earn them again. That's because we believe service is continuous. It's not a "one-and-done." We need to continuously try to achieve great service and to recognize it when we see it.

That's also why we don't have an employee-of-the-month program. If you put someone on a pedestal, they're guaranteed to fall off, or get knocked off, at some point. However, we do strongly encourage informal recognitions like, "We're having doughnuts today because Linda was so great last month, filling in for so many people in a pinch." This kind of spontaneous recognition is a huge morale booster, and what does it cost, twenty bucks?

DISCIPLINE

Of course, there are times when employees' behavior falls short of excellence. In such cases, our corrective action always starts with what we call a coaching, as I've mentioned before. A coaching is a nondisciplinary interaction—although we do document it so that, if necessary, we can say, "Hmm, I thought we talked about this on June 12."

If the problem behavior continues or resurfaces, we escalate to, "Okay, we spoke about this already, so it seems you're *choosing* to behave this way. Next we're going to give you a formal verbal warning. That will be the first stage of our progressive discipline program. It will go into your file. You may have union representation when we discuss it, but we're telling you now that the behavior is unwanted. After this warning, we expect to never discuss this issue again."

The next stage is a written notice: "Okay, now we're telling you in writing, which is step two in our disciplinary program. Please tell us now if there's something you don't understand or if you need further training or mentorship. Otherwise, if you continue to do this, it will lead to further discipline, including, perhaps, termination."

So, we root our feedback in mentorship that is firm, specific, and instructional in nature, and then we hold our people accountable in progressive ways. We vastly prefer to reward people for good behavior than to discipline people for poor behavior, but our team leaders need to understand that if they enable one person to be a subpar performer, they're telling everyone else they're working too hard. Occasionally an unpleasant conversation is required.

If you are not clear with discipline, you will spend 80 percent of your time dealing with negative behaviors. But if your discipline is clear and direct, you will have a stronger culture for it.

SALES READINESS—THE ULTIMATE MEASURE OF EXCELLENCE

As I've said before, everyone in our company is in sales. It is the job of every team member to fulfill the promises made by the sales and marketing team and to embody the values the company espouses. So the true measure of staff excellence is to see your entire team consistently behaving in ways that *sell the brand*. In other words, you could bring a prospective customer into your department or area, without any advance warning, and feel confident that your team will behave in a caring, attentive, and professional way. The extent to which you believe your team is sales ready at a moment's notice is an excellent measure of how much or how little work you need to do in upgrading your team.

STAFF DEVELOPMENT AND PROMOTION

A major aspect of creating staff excellence in any organization is, of course, to recognize talent, develop it, and allow people to contribute to the company at their highest possible level. One of the trickiest aspects of this process, especially in a care-centric business like ours, is to distinguish those employees who can and should advance from those who perhaps should not.

ADVANCEMENT ISN'T FOR EVERYONE

There is a persistent myth in business that everyone wants to advance. This is not true, nor should it be. The fact is that not everyone in your organization should want to be the CEO. That's not everyone's calling. It's good to have a *mix* of talent—some folks who are task oriented and others who are growth oriented. You can't have an entire hive of queen bees. Some have to be "worker bees" and happy to be so.

I use the term *worker bee* meaning no disparagement whatsoever. Some of the most valuable people in our organization are those who excel in the role they're in and are happy to be there. These people are self-motivated. They are glad to come to work. They've created relationships they love. They are great with residents and teammates alike. When you talk about leadership opportunities with these folks, they're not interested. They don't want to manage people. They love what they're doing. In many cases they may desire more *knowledge* so they can become even better at their jobs, but they're not gunning for a corner office.

When my managers tell me about one of these great people on their team, the first thing I ask is, "Are we at risk of losing them? Is there anything we can do to make them less likely to be a flight risk?" It's important to reward these satisfied, excellent performers *within the context* of their present roles (rather than by dangling promotions at them). Here is where frequent appreciation is critical—shout-outs, service ribbons, and informal thank-yous. You also want to offer these valued folks opportunities to develop their skills without pressuring them to leave their current roles. This might involve offering them training that enables them to be more effective within the role they are currently performing. One way we do this is by conducting twice-a-year "internal trade shows" in which staffers learn more about best practices and state-of-the-art developments within their disciplines—we'll talk about these in a later chapter.

Nowadays, given the tight labor market, it is also important to recognize and appreciate the "Steady Eddies"—those employees who may not be *standouts* but who show up every day and do good work. You need to say thank you to these people—not for being extraordinary but just for being steady, reliable, and consistent. If you don't find creative ways to appreciate the Steady Eddies, they can walk out the door and get a job across the street.

TAKING TALENT TO THE NEXT LEVEL

Equally valuable are those employees who *are* advance minded. It's important to be aware of who these people are and to talk with them often about their career goals. Many ambitious Millennials, for example, have a two-year timeline for every job they take. They're always looking up at the next rung of the ladder. It's important to not only offer these people experiences that enhance their résumés but also to give them a chance to advance within the organization, whenever possible. That means talking to them often. If you're not talking to your talent frequently and authentically, they'll just leave when a better opportunity pops up.

In our organization, we have about a 30 percent internal promotion record. Some of this is a result of our Seeds program, which helps us identify emerging talent and formally mentor them. For some this might involve individual coaching or company-paid courses at a local college or university. In other cases, it might mean cross-training the person—taking them out of their own department and giving them some exposure in other areas.

Similar to the way new hires shadow seasoned employees, we might take an existing employee and have them shadow people in other departments so they can learn about other jobs and how these jobs relate to one another. We might put someone, for example, on our concierge desk where they meet and greet people. We might put them in the dining room as a server. We might have them shadow a top leader. In this way a promising employee gains a more holistic view of our business.

One of our youngest, and best, general managers, for example, started out her Seasons career as a food server. She then went into the dietary department and became a Red Seal chef, and from there she went on to become the business manager. Soon she became interested in applying for the general manager's job, and we said, "You're not ready for that job, because every general manager has to know how to ask for the check. They have to know how to drive consensus and what good marketing and sales looks like."

So our answer to her wasn't no; it was not yet. We switched her over to sales. Not her first love, but within a year she had filled every vacancy in the home. And so when the general manager opportunity came open, she was the logical choice, even though she didn't have a lot of experience leading people. To ensure her success, we set up a mentorship arrangement where she received ongoing support from key members of our senior leadership team. And now this woman, who is not thirty yet, is one of our strongest leaders.

We would much rather promote people from within—people who understand our culture and service expectations—than bring people from outside and start from scratch.

IT'S ALL ABOUT RELATIONSHIPS

The key to creating and maintaining staff excellence comes down to relationships more than anything else. (Sound familiar?) Because when you have strong relationships—between staff and residents, among team members, and between management and staff—you have goodwill. And where goodwill exists, care expands exponentially.

BETWEEN STAFF AND RESIDENTS

Developing customer relationships is a major part of what the frontline staff does every day, but I especially love it when I see members of management and the non-direct-care teams getting out of their offices and talking to the residents. At homes where this happens regularly, there is a family feeling from top to bottom.

Recently, I stayed for lunch at one of our homes, and grilled cheese and tomato soup was the main menu offering. It was not— let's put it this way—a thrilling culinary excursion: white bread, American cheese, canned soup. The residents seemed to be enjoying themselves, but I was a bit underwhelmed with the fare, so I spoke to the chef. "Is this something the residents really love?" I asked.

The chef said, "I've tried making tomato soup from scratch, I've tried using artisan bread, I've tried using various kinds of international cheese. And when I do, I always get an earful. The folks here are very specific about what they want with this lunch. It's got to be Campbell's soup from a can, and it's got to be American cheese on white bread. To them, it's childhood, it's comfort food, it's home. They'd eat it twice a week if they could."

I stood corrected. I could see that the chef had come by her knowledge through developing a relationship with the residents.

Having real, caring relationships between staff and residents makes a world of difference in the quality of staff service. It allows staff to tailor their services and offerings to customers' specific tastes and personalities. And it allows residents to become involved with residential life in more meaningful ways, such as growing an herb garden for the kitchen staff to use or playing classical guitar for the weekly wine bar.

BETWEEN COMPANY AND STAFF

If you wish to have an excellent staff that provides great customer care, you need to care for your staff as well. That means developing real relationships among the staff members themselves and between management and employees. At Seasons much of this is accomplished via our relationship-based culture, but here are some additional things we do ...

To promote stronger intrastaff relationships, we put extra funds in our managers' budgets and encourage them to take the staff out of the work environment at least once a quarter. This might be just a bowling trip or an apple-picking excursion or a pizza night in a local restaurant. We know that when people relate to each other on a personal level, they're more likely to help each other on a professional level. They're more apt to recognize when someone's having a bad day and offer support and empathy. Connecting employees to each other on the most mundane level makes them more likely to help each other when things go badly.

We care about our employees' wellness and physical/mental health too. We try, for example, not to burn people out. Sometimes when we have staff vacancies, we must rely on the existing staff to pick up extra shifts. But we have to be extremely careful not to overwork people or to keep staff vacancies open too long.

We've negotiated a preferential membership rate for all our employees at a national fitness chain. We do annual wellness and health events, such as weight-loss and smoking-cessation challenges. We also offer a confidential EAP (employee assistance program). This is a resource leaders can offer to team members. The EAP gives employees access to counseling, legal resources, extra medical support, and more, for themselves or their family. The company pays for it, and we don't know who receives the services. Totally anonymous.

For managers who are important to us but who might be struggling with some leadership issues, we sometimes provide an outside career coach. The leader can talk with their coach about any difficulties they're having. Again, it's all confidential, so they can talk freely about their bosses and admit to weaknesses they wouldn't be comfortable talking about in-house.

For valued employees who might be dealing with major medical issues, such as cancer or surgery needs, we will sometimes offer to seek out a third-party opinion and give the employee added support on obtaining the best care possible. This might include providing additional MRIs and consultations and/or connections to top oncologists or radiologists. This add-on can be tremendously expensive, so we can't do it for everyone, but for people who are suffering performance challenges due only to health reasons, it's the right thing to do. Also, as a side bonus, it buys us an astonishing amount of goodwill. I've had people on the verge of tears, saying, "You would do this for *me*?" These people remain loyal forever.

The ability to care for our people in personal ways is one of the reasons I don't want to be the *biggest* company; I want to be the best. Once you become a giant operation that has a book of HR policies thicker than the Bible, it's difficult to be great. And so for us it's important that we never lose sight of the fact that our people are our product. Treating them well is critical.

The flip side of that is that if you're not special as an employee, you can't stay. Sorry, but that's just the way it is in our business culture. Staff excellence is job one.

BUT WAIT—BEFORE YOU GO!

Here are a few final thoughts about creating staff excellence:

- If you are fair and consistent with discipline, within a culture of excellence, you'll end up with a team that does most of your discipline for you. If and when an underperformer joins their department, the team will self-police. They'll take that person off to the side and say, "If you keep this behavior up, you're not going to enjoy what's coming next."

- When teams struggle, it's usually because they're working as individuals. When teams really hit their stride, it's because they're working as a team, sharing the success and the pain with one another.

- Storytelling is an essential part of hiring, onboarding, training, and promoting. Always be telling stories that capture the essence of your brand. People internalize stories and remember them long after the instructional stuff has been forgotten.

CHAPTER SEVEN

LEADERSHIP EXCELLENCE

nd now, the final part of our value chain—actually, it's the first part, if you'll recall. And in many ways it's the most important. The number one way we create the care that is our main value add is by constantly working on leadership excellence. In a nutshell, to have an organization that cares and excels, you must have leaders who care and excel. And to achieve *that*, you must make an extraordinary investment in your current and future leaders.

The timing of this chapter happens to be fortuitous. As I sit down to write it, I have just returned from our annual leadership conference. This conference is a major event in the Seasons calendar. We invest a

> To have an organization that cares and excels, you must have leaders who care and excel.

lot of time, care, and money in it. And, as with the caring acts that occur every day at our residences, the results of the conference are nontransactional. That is, we can't count on a direct, measurable return on this huge annual investment we make—but to me it is the most important thing we do, organizationally, every year. It is the heart of our leadership development.

This year, we took two hundred of our leaders to Whistler, British Columbia, a beautiful ski town nestled in the mountains, and treated them to a great service experience at the Fairmont hotel. The purpose of the annual conference is always multifold. Partly, it's a reward for our people. It's a way for us to care for them. They get a chance to spend time in a beautiful location and have some fun and relaxation. We offer activities like ziplining, river rafting, or luxuriating in a Scandinavian spa. And we pay for everything. It's our way to thank our leadership team and to renew their faith in the company.

The second reason for the conference is so our people can experience what it's like to be the recipient of excellent service. We chose the Fairmont this year because it is a top brand that's well aligned with our philosophy of hospitality. On at least one evening of each conference, the main leaders also play host to the departmental leaders at some of the best restaurants around, so they can connect with each other and also enjoy some great food and service experiences together. We want our leaders to be inspired by the service they receive and committed to bringing new service ideas back to Seasons. We want them to have some shared experiences that can serve as benchmarks.

Thirdly, and most importantly, we want to challenge and stimulate our leaders. Each year we present a series of top-notch keynote speakers that help us set our leadership agenda for the upcoming year. So it's not just about the parties. It's work too. This year, we had an especially strong lineup of four speakers, each of whom would have been worthy of an entire conference. I'll talk about them all in a minute, but first I want to tell you about a seemingly silly aspect of the conference that really struck me this year.

PASSION IN A TOGA

Every year, as part of the conference, we run some kind of fun competition among the leadership teams of the various Seasons communities. One year it might be a songwriting competition for a Culture That Rocks theme; another year it might be a dance contest. There's no financial benefit to winning, only bragging rights. This year, someone (not I) decided we would have a toga party with a prize going to the team with the most outrageous costumes. Dumb idea? Sure, it always is. But that's okay. The idea is to put our leaders in a new environment, unshackle their imaginations, and let them have a great time.

Every year, the competition is ferocious, and this year was no different. The winner of the toga contest was the leadership team from our Stony Creek community—its head of dietary, head of housekeeping, business, sales, general manager, and so on. What did they do to win? They painted themselves silver and gray from head to toe, like stone statues from a Greek temple. Then they proceeded to sneak into the main party room early, before everyone arrived, and stood perfectly still, eyes closed, for thirty minutes. As everyone filed into the room, we all thought someone in the company had hired actors to play these statues—until the Stony Creek team members "came alive" and revealed themselves. We were blown away.

Stony Creek has won this award three years running. So what? It's just a dumb contest, right? Well, yes and no. As I've mentioned before, Seasons does a company-wide annual survey of its frontline staff. Stony Creek is the only community I've ever seen in my entire career that has had a 100 percent participation rate in their staff survey. They also have the highest *satisfaction* rate among their frontline staff, and they have the highest satisfaction rate among residents.

Coincidence? I don't think so. As I thought about what the connection might be between these silly stone statues and Stony Creek's off-the-charts satisfaction levels, I realized there is a fierce competitive spirit that drives the Stony Creek team (and our other teams as well). And it's far more than just a zeal to win bragging rights. It's a reflection of the *passion* of the team. And passion is the X factor that makes for excellence in leadership.

Like the caring quality in frontline staff, passion can't be taught or manufactured, and it can't be faked. But it is essential in a great company, and it flows down into everything its people do.

Passion, in fact, is the *way* leaders care. Leaders don't typically get involved in the direct care aspects of the hospitality business. Though it's great when they take the time to engage with customers, leaders aren't the ones who offer Mrs. Smith the special slice of coffee cake or help Sam jump out of a plane. For leaders in our business, care shows up as *passion*—passion about the company and its purpose, passion about its customers, passion about excelling.

When leaders have passion, they inspire caring in their teams.

FOUR ESSENTIAL PASSIONS

The passion shown for something as silly as a toga contest was especially fitting for this year's leadership conference, because it happened that the theme of the conference was passion—passion in four key leadership areas:

- passion for brand

- passion for customer

- passion for service

- passion for self

We planned the conference as a way to inspire these four passions in our leaders, and now these four passions will be the theme of our upcoming leadership year. They will serve as our building blocks as we try to grow and improve the organization over the next twelve months.

As it turns out, these four passions also make a great basis for a chapter about leadership excellence.

Let's look at the way our four excellent speakers illustrated key aspects of these four passions and the way we plan to use their messages to strengthen our passion as a leadership team over the coming year.

PASSION FOR BRAND

Jonathan Mildenhall was the first of our speakers. As you may know, he is the author of a couple of great books, but he is most noteworthy for being chief marketing officer for Coca-Cola for a dozen years and for launching the Airbnb brand. Both of these huge global brands embrace exceptional principles, and both have faced challenges to these principles.

Coca-Cola has always stood out as a brand that transcends money and even its own soft drink products. Coke tries to convey a *feeling*— of joy, togetherness, and unity. Many of its top ad campaigns over the years have involved sharing a Coke with those who may be different from you. This kind of messaging, needless to say, can face some major challenges in a world as starkly divided as ours. And responding to these challenges requires bold leadership and risk taking. For example, (before Mildenhall's tenure) Coca-Cola was the first advertiser to depict black and white kids having a Coke together. Coke did this in the South at a time when there were still segregated benches. When Martin Luther King won the Nobel Prize in 1964, Coca-Cola took a major stand by hosting a highly controversial *integrated* dinner in his honor. When MLK was assassinated, Coca-Cola sent a private jet to pick up his remains and bring him back to Atlanta, where the company's main headquarters are, and paid for the funeral.

Jonathan talked about a campaign he himself launched between India and Pakistan in which a new technology was employed to allow people from these two conflicting nations to connect with each other via their shared love of Coca-Cola. This was an amazing opportunity to leverage a brand in a way that was not transactional in nature. It was entirely about how you make people feel. Very, very powerful.

Later, Mildenhall had an early experience with the Airbnb brand where some of its landlords began to discriminate in terms of whom they would rent to. Some refused to rent to gay people, others were discriminating racially, and so on. So Airbnb, which was still in its formative years, had to make a tough decision about how to handle this. Its leadership under Mildenhall said, "We're not a platform that says home is only where the whites are; home is wherever *you* are. And that needs to mean the same for anyone and everyone."

So they pulled 25 percent of their leasable space, based on those kinds of discrimination policies. This was at a time when the business really needed to grow, and the board and private equity partners were probably saying, "Are you crazy?" But the CEO stood firm and said, "This is what we stand for. Trust me. Over time this will work. But right now the smartest thing for us to do is shrink." They did, and subsequently they had hundredfold growth over the next five to seven years. But this result was by no means guaranteed when Mildenhall made his stand. He took a risk—but a risk *on behalf* of the brand rather than a risk *of* the brand. Key difference.

THE TAKEAWAY

Jonathan Mildenhall's talk was inspirational. What we hope our leadership team will take away from it is an understanding of how important passion and commitment to the brand is. We want our leaders to feel empowered to take risks on behalf of our brand. Even if we don't face major challenges this year or next year, our industry is continually evolving and in constant flux. Sooner or later, some or all of our leaders will be in a position where they'll need to take a risky stand to protect the brand, and we want them to know we will be behind them.

Risks don't always come in a socially controversial form, as they did for Mildenhall. Sometimes they come in the form of a risky investment that is made with the hope that the brand will benefit down the line. An example of this is our leadership conference itself, which costs the company a huge amount of money and has no guaranteed, specific payoff. It is an act of pure faith in our brand. Another example is a new high-tech piece of cooking equipment we're investing in for some of our homes. This beast is far more than an oven. It can cook numerous different foods at different temperatures and then hold each of them at the right temperature for hours. It is also Wi-Fi enabled and keeps inventory for restocking. It is many times more expensive than a conventional stove, but we hope it will allow our chefs to spend more time cooking and less time administrating. Because the oven takes care of the mundane stuff, the chefs can now focus on making pies and soups and sauces from scratch, which we believe will please our customers and enhance our brand. It's a financial risk, but it's one we'll take every time.

We have always worked toward having great brand passion at Seasons, and we have been successful so far. As I've noted, we have many employees who would "wear the tattoo" if they could. But this kind of passion must be continually stoked at the leadership level.

PASSION FOR CUSTOMER

Our second keynote speaker was author and TED Talker Ashton Applewhite. She is one of today's most prominent voices in the anti-ageism movement. In her talk, she pointed out that ageism is one of the last "isms" that has been allowed to persist, and it is based on myths. Nearly all of us, even those in businesses that serve seniors, have fears and prejudices about aging that simply aren't valid. For example, we imagine that most elders end up being infirm and needing care, when in fact only 4 percent of elders go into nursing homes. We think of depression as increasing with age, when in fact the opposite is true—people are happiest toward the beginning and end of life. Dementia is on the decrease, not the increase. And so on.

As a result of the false stereotypes of aging, our culture views aging as something shameful and problematic rather than as a natural part of the life cycle. We sell products to "cure" the natural signs of aging and drugs to treat the aging brain. But such products only increase the misunderstanding that aging is a problem to be fixed or hidden away in shame.

Ageism, like other prejudices, is rooted in the concept of "othering," says Applewhite. When we assign certain characteristics to seniors as a group, we're saying they are different from us. And so we feel justified in treating them differently. We in the senior residential industry are not immune from this. Whenever we refer to a resident diminutively as Sweetie or Young Lady; whenever we remove adult choices from them, such as the freedom to have a drink or express themselves sexually; whenever we offer them childlike entertainment choices or bland, tasteless food, we infantilize them. Even when we label our product "independent supportive living," what we're really saying is that people who live in our communities are *less* independent, less able than the general population.

Applewhite powerfully reinforced the idea that human beings continue to grow and develop right until the end of life and need to be treated with respect and a full range of adult choices. We in the senior services industry must consider reexamining why we do the things we do and even the vernacular we use every day.

THE TAKEAWAY

Though Seasons continually examines its premises about aging and the way we think of elderly consumers, Applewhite's message was a powerful one for all of us. We need to become *even more* passionate about discovering who our customers really are—beyond whatever stereotypes we may be holding in our minds. Because those prejudices, to whatever extent we hold them, block us from seeing what our clients' real needs might be.

A passionate desire to connect with the truth of our customers' lives will change the kinds of services we offer, the way we offer them, the way we market our services, and the

> A passionate desire to connect with the truth of our customers' lives will change the kinds of services we offer, the way we offer them, the way we market our services, and the kinds of responses we try to elicit from prospective customers—now and in the future.

kinds of responses we try to elicit from prospective customers—now and in the future.

One profound reason for becoming more passionate about the customer is the ever-increasing wave of baby boomers that will be moving into retirement homes over the next couple of decades. The boomers are a generation that is used to dictating what the market provides, not settling for whatever services the market offers them. They view aging in a completely new way and will not put up with many of the standards and practices that exist in senior services today. Unless we—as a brand, as leaders, and as a staff—are absolutely passionate about discovering who our new customers are and what they want, we will become irrelevant.

PASSION FOR SERVICE

Our next speaker was Clarence McCloud, who was the global concierge and Gold-Floor-experience leader for the Fairmont chain of hotels. He is currently the only "guilded butler" in North America, which means he was trained by England's royal staff in the Victorian style of butlering and is a member of the Guild of Professional English Butlers. He has served Queen Elizabeth II, Susan Sarandon and other stars, and a number of world leaders. He has established butler programs in countries all around the world.

If you have ever had the opportunity to stay on a Fairmont Gold Floor, then you know it is a bit of a butler-like experience. They know your name, they know your drink, and they provide a dedicated concierge throughout your stay. Fairmont Gold offers things like private check-in, afternoon canapés, and a "pillow concierge." So it's an amazing experience. And McLeod staffed it and trained virtually every butler that serves the Gold Floor concierge service experience. He's a great guy with a burning passion for service.

Clarence talked about going above and beyond expectations to create extraordinary moments. He is fearless about trying to make something special happen for guests. For example, he once flew in grapes from a private vineyard to make a guest's breakfast complete. It became clear to us that Fairmont uses principles very close to our Connect, Care, Change model. Their service is built on the idea that you must know who your customer is and desire to surpass their expectations. If you connect and you care enough, you can make a significant change to someone's day, someone's life, and someone's impression of your business and brand.

THE TAKEAWAY

McLeod's ultrahigh commitment to service, based on a model like ours, was extremely affirming and inspiring for our leaders. It made us think about being more creative and personalized in the way we deliver service. Of course, at a Fairmont, you have only a few days to make someone's experience amazing. We have 365 days, so we have a different view of how to create wow moments. We want our people to be fundamentally great at the basics, because we aim to create a *cumulative experience* of care.

But McLeod's talk really confirmed for us that we're on the right track with our high standards and attention to detail. Someone from the outside might think these standards excessive. For example, we put a mirror in every one of our staff rooms, with an outline of what the uniform looks like. It shows where the name tag goes. If the employee wears a hat or an apron, it shows how that should sit. Each time a staffer leaves the break room, they look at themselves in the mirror, and if they don't reflect what that outline shows, they're not "show ready."

This type of passion for service was validated by learning that our service philosophy is echoed by one of the continent's leading service authorities. McLeod made us want to try even harder.

PASSION FOR SELF

Our final speaker was as impressive as the first three: Greg Wells. He is a physiologist as well as an accomplished swimmer, best-selling author, and expert on fitness and wellness. He trains people for job performance, self-improvement, and professional competition. He has a long list of Olympic athletes he has helped coach, not just technically but also from a perspective of psychology, sleep, nutrition, training, and optimal performance. He's often brought in to help pro sports teams change their culture regarding performance and wellness.

His latest book is *The Ripple Effect*, and he talked about the central idea from that book, which is simply this: If you take care of yourself—by sleeping a little more, moving a little more, eating a little better, and thinking a little better (e.g., worrying less)—the positive effects begin to snowball, and your life and performance notably improve. Without extreme effort.

Wells talked about some simple but deliberate things we can all do to start the ripple effect. For example: Turn off your electronic devices an hour before bed, and read a book. Use caffeine as an occasional stimulant to help improve focus and performance, not as a daily crutch. Practice gratitude every day by keeping a journal of things you are grateful for. Walk fifteen minutes a day; no need to climb Mount Everest. Taking small, but intentional, steps like these is doable for everyone, but the ripple effects can be profound.

THE TAKEAWAY

The audience resonated with Greg's simple but inspiring message, and I think we all walked away with the idea that becoming improved human beings doesn't happen by dumb luck. It comes as a result of making good, sensible choices and putting in a little effort. It's not about breaking world records; it's about incremental steps. It's about continuing to build on your own success. Have a goal, work toward it steadily, and forgive yourself if you fail. Don't punish yourself to the point where all you see is the negative; just say, "I'm going to make better choices going forward. I'm going to play more with my kids. I'm going to watch less TV. I'm going to read a book on self-improvement."

We don't yet know how Greg's insight and inspiration will play out for us, but he definitely planted the seeds for creating a new health and wellness challenge in each of our communities—among the leaders, the staff, and the customers. Because a healthy workforce is a workforce that comes to work happier and more energetic. And a healthy customer is one who is more engaged.

PASSION FOR LEADERSHIP EXCELLENCE

So, passion is the essence of leadership excellence, and it was the theme for this year's conference. We did everything we could, by way of the conference, to fire up the passion of our leadership team in these four key areas. And now it's up to us to reinforce that message every month for the next year and to use it as a building block for reinforcing some of the leadership qualities we want them to focus on.

Passion is a topic I would have written about regardless of the fortuitous theme of the conference. When leaders have passion, you can see it reflected in the communities they lead. When I enter our Stony Creek community, for example, the residents look energetic and well groomed, the staff look happy to see me rather than fearful, and the place looks clean and welcoming. It glows. The passion of the leaders shines through.

Passion is what allows leaders to lead by influence and inspiration rather than by authority. It is what gives leaders the resilience to overcome setbacks and periods of slow or no growth. It is the intangible "magic" that flows from the top of the organization all the way down to the smile on the face of the frontline staff person who greets Mrs. Smith with her piping hot coffee.

This is why the leader of a great organization must commit to instilling a passion for excellence in his or her entire leadership team.

* * *

Leadership excellence leads to staff excellence. Staff excellence leads to exceptional customer experiences. Exceptional customer experiences lead to fuller consensus. And in our business, it's that final percentage of consensus that contains all our profits. That's because most of our costs are fixed. Whether we're at 80 percent or 100 percent occupancy, we have the same number of staff; we pay the same utilities and taxes; we have essentially the same upkeep costs. So it's that final 10 or 20 percent where we thrive financially. And the way we fill those spaces is by caring for customers and making them feel at home. See how it all comes together?

BUT WAIT—BEFORE YOU GO!

A few more ideas to ponder regarding leadership excellence:

- Serving on boards is a great way to polish your own leadership excellence and to stay up to speed on changes in your industry.

- The Jack Welsh approach is to lose your bottom 10 percent every year and build the best leadership team possible, and that's okay. But the *top* 10 percent are your keepers. You've got to give them something they want to stick around for.

- A great leader makes it look easy for those under them to be successful. That's because a great leader bulldozes the obstacles out of the way and deals with all the problems no one else wants to face.

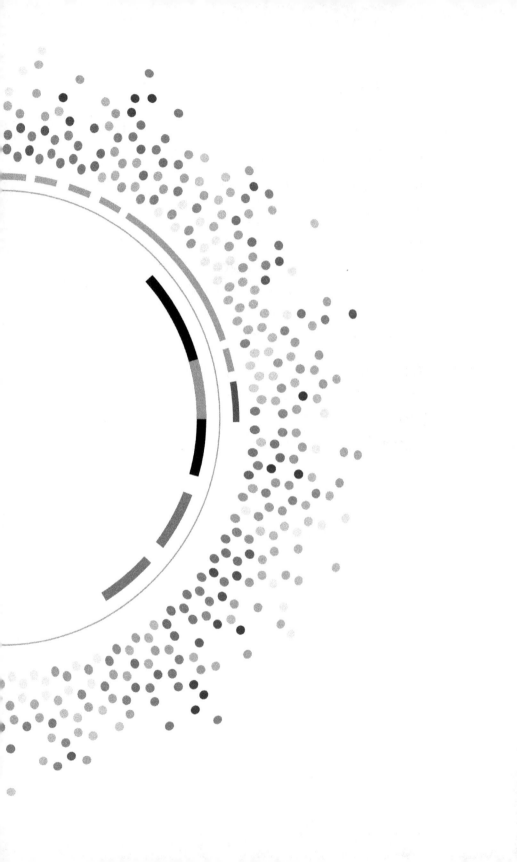

PART III:
CHANGING

The third of our Three Cs, Change, is the ultimate purpose of the other two Cs.

We live in a dynamic, changing world. The economy is constantly changing. Customers and their needs are constantly changing. Employees and their needs are constantly changing. The competition is constantly changing—offering new models, new services, new products. The investment community is constantly changing.

And so a vital business must be constantly responding *to change. It must also be constantly* creating *change of its own. Business should be a verb, not a noun.*

In our business, we're trying to change lives *for the better, one moment at a time. But we're also trying to build a better staff, create better business models and services, and generate higher profits. All of these things require a passionate daily commitment to change, as a business. Which means your culture must have change embedded in it.*

Change is not some empty business platitude or inconvenience to be dealt with; it is your *reason for getting out of bed in the morning. Every day, as you enter your office, your dominant motivating thought should be, "What can I improve today? What can I change for the better?"*

CHAPTER EIGHT

WHY EMBRACING CHANGE IS VITAL

Y ou've probably read the statistics. Twenty percent of businesses fail within the first two years, 45 percent fail within the first five years, and 65 percent fail within the first ten years. Fully 75 percent of the businesses that were around only fifteen years ago have disappeared.[6]

For virtually every business that fails, you can say the same thing: somewhere along the line, the need to change and/or the *opportunity* for change presented itself, and the company did not adequately respond. On the other hand, for every business that *thrives* over time, you can say the opposite: they looked with open eyes at the changing landscape around them, identified some competitive advantages they could seize, and acted on them. They stayed *abreast* or *ahead* of change instead of *behind* it. They innovated.

---

6   https://www.investopedia.com/financial-edge/1010/top-6-reasons-new-businesses-fail.aspx.

Innovation is the creative response to change. Innovation is a necessity for long-term success. Businesses that do not innovate become more and more commodity driven—that is, they offer essentially the same products as everyone else. They end up trying to compete on price, and eventually all they do is focus on costs. They find themselves becoming less and less relevant, they have less cash on hand, and it becomes harder and harder for them to reinvest in new opportunities. Profits erode, which means lower returns. Investors eventually move on.

> Innovation is the creative response to change. Innovation is a necessity for long-term success.

Conversely, a business that really *embraces* change in a leading way creates a powerful marketing opportunity for attracting both customers and employees. It also creates a powerful incentive for investors to keep that vital business in their portfolios.

Being change driven is a cultural trait every business should foster and incubate. This requires both an *external* and an *internal* focus. You must be keenly aware of changes that are happening "out there"—in the economy, in your business sector (and other sectors), in your customer base, in technology, in tastes, in society as a whole. And you must be nimble enough *internally* to change your products and services in response.

THE CHANGING CUSTOMER

Whatever business you are in, you are in customer service. And the customers you are serving are in a constant state of dynamic change. Their tastes and needs are changing, their economic circumstances are changing, and their life conditions are changing. They are aging and learning. In order to keep winning new customers and retaining existing ones, you *must* be enthusiastically tuned in to the ways in which your customers are changing.

In our business, customer change occurs on different levels. First, there are generational changes that reflect the tastes and behaviors of large waves of people. For example, we are currently servicing the Silent Generation. This includes the tail end of those who lived through the Great Depression. Character-wise, these folks are not complainers; they're savers, coupon clippers, hard workers. They're resilient, but they don't pound their fists on tables. They're not activists. They grew up in an era of fewer choices, less technology, less economic certainty, greater trust in authority. They value the simple things. They're more apt to accept the services they're offered and do what the doctor tells them.

The coming wave is the baby boomers. The leading edge of this group contains the first generational activists. They protested wars, marched against racism, and fought for women's rights. They were all about causes and change. Many of them are now affluent; they've had the time to save and inherit money. They're very choice driven. They want to be an active part of their own medical care. They work out, they're disciplined and focused. They also drink good booze, eat good food, smoke pot, and listen to rock and roll. They will require a whole different level of services, and we're already thinking about some major ways we will need to change in response to them.

The senior population also changes because of shifting life needs, and these changes can happen fast. I was recently talking, for example, to a colleague whose in-laws sold their home and moved into a town house on the campus of a retirement community. At the time of the move, they were still driving their own car, doing their own shopping and cooking, and living an independent lifestyle.

About a year later, cognitive changes required them to stop driving and move to an assisted-living apartment on campus. It wasn't long before the husband required increased medical care, and so he moved into the nursing care wing, where his wife was permitted to join him. He died about six months later, and then the wife began to experience worsening Alzheimer's symptoms. She began wandering the streets at three a.m. thinking it was time for church. The staff and family decided to transfer her to the secure memory care unit. From there, physical health issues necessitated inpatient treatment at an affiliated hospital. Discharged with a terminal diagnosis, she returned to the nursing wing, where an in-house hospice program was arranged for her. All of this occurred within a *five-year period*.

That's a massive amount of change. And a massive amount of changing *service*.

As a provider, the more you are able to observe these changes and respond to them with tailored services, the better it is for everyone. The customer gains the peace of mind of knowing they won't need to move to a new community every time their needs change. The business gains the ability to retain a valuable customer long term.

Customers are always evolving. Their needs, tastes, and situations are ever changing. So we who serve them must be constantly changing too. We must compete for the hearts and minds of those who spend their discretionary dollars with us. And it isn't pocket change we're talking about here. An eighty-year-old who spends three years in one of our retirement communities will spend more with us than they spent on their first house. So customer retention is a big deal, business-wise. Which means we need to find ways to maintain a longer life cycle—a longer relationship—with our existing residents. Which means we *must* be fine-tuned to their ever-changing needs, and we must offer changing services to address those needs.

Change is the opportunity to serve in new ways. Every business should burn these words onto a plaque.

CHANGING EXTERNAL REALITIES

Change is the opportunity to serve in new ways.

Changes in your customer base are just one of many external changes that must be weighed and balanced when making internal changes to your company. This might seem obvious, but again, the reason so many businesses fail is that they put on blinders. They don't fully take in the changes happening in the world around them. And so they cling—consciously or unconsciously—to ideas that are no longer optimal.

INDUSTRY CHANGES AND COMPETITION

The competitive landscape is always in flux. Everyone in your industry is scrambling to gain an edge. And try as you might, it's not possible for you to lead the charge in *every* area. Sometimes a competitor has a new idea first. You need to be nimble enough to change your models and services whenever a better idea comes along. Sometimes this requires a period of pause and reflection first. You must observe how well the change is working for the competitor. And then you must look for a way to iterate on that change so as to offer something even better.

In our business, we operate in micromarkets. Each micromarket has competitors that change their business offerings in different ways. We strive to be sure we are always responding to each changing landscape—and that we're carving out a piece for ourselves that is unique enough to buy us a long-term, differentiated competitive advantage.

For instance, if we operate in a marketplace that has a lot of independent, supportive living and we suddenly find ourselves facing price and occupancy struggles, we might say, "What if we repurpose part of our building and turn it into a secure environment for memory care clients? Will that solve our occupancy issues and create a sustainable edge for us?" If the answer looks like yes, we'll pull the trigger—we'll spend the $2 million needed to retrofit the building.

THE ECONOMY AND OTHER GLOBAL FORCES

Of course, even the above type of decision must be weighed in the context of larger changes taking place on a national and global level, such as changes in the economy, in health care, in the regulatory environment, and in the housing and construction industries.

For example, as I write this, we are in the middle of one of the tightest labor markets ever seen in North America. In the United States, there is a historically low sub–3 percent employment rate, which is not good for employers. We have similar problems in Canada. Our rate is sitting at twenty-five-year lows. This is problematic for several reasons, one of which is that it drives inflation.

This can affect our business strategy. For example, you might wonder why we don't just build memory care units into every new project we launch. Well, the labor shortage has pushed the cost of construction up 20 to 30 percent over the last three years, far outstripping our ability to charge more to customers and catch up to the increasing cost. So we must change and adapt.

Maybe what we'll do in this case is hold off on building those memory care units. Instead, we'll offer a lighter service model we can market to a younger, more independent senior who doesn't need the more intensive services yet. (It's easier to *staff* this lighter model, too, in tight labor conditions.) Then we'll keep an eye on our customers' changing needs. Maybe in five to seven years, the need for memory care will be stronger and the labor market pendulum will have swung the other way. So we'll retrofit our building later, instead of doing it today.

The labor market also affects the kinds of services we offer. Though we might have a zillion great ideas for offering better care and convenience to our residents, right now there aren't enough workers available to deliver all those services. So for now we might need to rely on innovation and technology more than warm bodies as we try to upgrade our offerings.

TECHNOLOGY

Technology, of course, is another huge force driving change in almost every industry, including ours. The changing ways in which smart, internet-enabled devices can interact with one another has created a fast-changing and unpredictable service market. No one in business can afford to be ignorant of these changes or to take an "old school," technophobic approach.

In recent years, for example, technology has changed to allow seniors to remain in their own homes longer. Emergency-alert pendants, internet-connected video cameras, medication management apps, vital-sign monitors, and other such devices provide a level of connectivity and security that can delay a senior's need for a more supported setting. This technology, in turn, affects the way we market our services to seniors and transition them into our communities. We also incorporate many of these new technologies into our homes as well, which changes the types of services we can offer and the types of clients that are appropriate for our various levels of care.

Technology now also allows us to collect a lot of information on every customer. This data potentially enables us to offer highly tailored services to clients and also to keep better track of their health. For example, we are currently switching to a new form of EHR (electronic health record) that will allow us to see emerging health patterns more clearly. When you combine EHRs with medical monitoring devices, and you add in our ability to do things like electronically monitor a client's gym usage, meal choices, and physical activity, you create the potential for a highly sophisticated system we could use to help clients live healthier and longer.

However, such information collecting must be weighed against privacy concerns. People don't like feeling "watched." Also, family members tend to be skeptical of data collecting. They know there's an economic incentive for us to collect more data, because then we can charge for new services the client may not need yet. So we have to walk a fine line between collecting data that will be used to take better care of folks and monetizing that service to an obnoxious degree. Changing *attitudes* about such matters are as important as changing technology.

When it comes to technology, it's important to keep up with changes in industries besides your own. For example, in our new buildings we recently switched to a keyless room entry system like those used in higher-end hotels. You just wave your fob near the door to gain entry. This allows us to control and keep track of who enters every room and when. It also gives our residents a better feeling of safety and security. And like anything else, that's an added value.

HOLISTIC WHENEVER POSSIBLE

The better you are able to see the changing world around you, the more holistic and workable solutions you can provide. It does no good to propose a brilliant new service if you won't be able to hire the staff to execute it or if it's going to be rendered obsolete in six months by changing technology. The best solutions take into consideration a wide range of evolving factors. By doing so, they solve multiple problems simultaneously.

Here are a few examples of changes we have recently made that work in a holistic way:

- In one of our communities, we were pretty good at taking care of high-acuity clients, but we needed to improve our bottom line, so we bought land adjacent to the property and built some townhomes. These are designed for people who still drive a car and cook their own meals. The new units allow us to attract a younger, more independent clientele. But they also double as a feeder system for the main community. When these residents' needs for services increase, they can just move into the central building.

- The high-tech oven I mentioned earlier allows for kitchen staff to spend less time on noncooking tasks so they can spend more time interacting with residents and creating home-style meals. It also generates a better product, which creates a better dining experience and allows us to market our food service more aggressively—which leads to better customer attraction and retention and a healthier bottom line.

- Because we have relatively fixed inventory and fixed cost structures, we're always looking for creative ways to generate extra income and offset cost increases. For example, we look for cell phone companies who want to rent space on our rooftops for putting antennas up. We are exploring solar power grids for our roofs. We recently converted all our buildings from incandescent lighting to LEDs. These changes allow us, in some cases, to mitigate rent increases, which in turn improves our relationships with residents.

- In some communities we are looking at creating an in-house grocery delivery service. In this way we can create another revenue stream for ourselves as well as a closer relationship with residents. We'll also gain the ability to look at independent residents' dietary habits firsthand. If a client suddenly stops eating, for example, we'll be alerted to this issue before further medical problems develop. Poor nutrition and hydration can lead to falls and hospitalization. Being involved with a client's groceries could give us a whole new window into their overall health and well-being.

It is the *embracing* of change on many levels that permits multi-dimensional solutions and exciting innovation to emerge.

THE CHANGING EMPLOYEE

Not only are your customers and business circumstances in a constant state of change; your employee base is always changing too. At the time of this writing, we are in a seller's market, employment-wise. Employ*ees* are the sellers and employ*ers* are the buyers. As employers, we must come up with competitive and creative ways to attract and retain staff. We talked about some of this already.

As with our customer base, some employee changes are generational. Millennials, for example, have a different collective view of work than previous generations. They are more mobile and entrepreneurial in their thinking. They don't seek out long-term relationships with a single employer, and they don't trust that employers really have their backs. They operate in shorter time frames. In their minds, a job is good for two years. After that, you'd better give them a new opportunity, or they'll be on to greener pastures.

Individual employees change over time too. They might be fine with a part-time, low-skill job when they're younger, but as they mature and their life conditions change—marriage, family, home ownership—they need better benefits, salaries, and opportunities. You need to have a way to accommodate these changes and create a flow of upward movement for staff.

WHY YOUR BUSINESS NEEDS TO GROW

This brings us to a reason for growing your business that we haven't discussed before. Even if you didn't care about generating more profits and higher returns, you would still need to grow your business for one simple reason: you need to provide growth opportunities to employees. If you want to retain great employees long term, you must offer them the potential for growth and advancement. Without such opportunities, employees stagnate and eventually leave. You lose your ability to attract the best and brightest—because no one wants to join a company that's a career dead end. The quality of your care then goes down, customers leave, and you enter a vicious cycle of decline.

Growth is healthy (provided it is done thoughtfully and organically).

EMPLOYEE GROWTH IS ALWAYS GOOD

At our company we are raving supporters of employee growth. Period. This means we do everything we can to foster growth within the company, but we are also comfortable with turnover. At Seasons, we have a low rate of turnover with our full-time employees but a high rate among part-time employees. That's because many of our part-timers start to desire full-time employment, and that's hard to obtain at a company where the full-timers don't want to leave! So we are perfectly fine when a part-timer uses the training we've given them to snag a full-time job somewhere else. We're happy for them— we truly are.

We have the same attitude about our valued full-timers. Sometimes a great employee feels a need to advance in a certain career direction at a certain speed, and we can't accommodate them at the time. We don't burn that bridge; instead, we try to help the person find their best opportunity elsewhere. We make calls; we advise them; we help them transition. We know there is a good chance that person will find their way back to us at some future point, with new skills and experiences and an even greater appreciation for our culture.

That very scenario has played out for us many times. For example, a general manager at one of our properties was a very ambitious person. She was a great clinician, and she was always looking for more growth, more responsibility. There came a point where we couldn't keep up with her drive. She left and took a regional role with a competitor. She hated it. Six months later, she knocked on our door and said, "Is there a way I could come back?" We found a role for her. That eventually developed into another opportunity for her to explore yet another company. She left again. Again the experience was not so rosy. She came back a second time and said, "Look, I really love this company and its culture. I would love to stay here on a long-term basis."

And so we created a regional clinical role that now oversees the entire company. And she's doing a terrific job for us in that role.

Someone who knows what it's like on the other side of the fence and comes back because they love your way of doing things is an extremely loyal employee and a powerful advocate for your culture.

Much more so than if they'd never left. Because they know the difference, having experienced it firsthand.

When it comes to employees, our attitude reflects the old saying, "If you love someone, set them free." We love our people, so we don't try to stifle them or hold them back. We champion their growth. That way, whether they come back to us or not, they remain an ally and a friend.

You might be thinking that training these people only to see them leave is a tremendous expense and a drain to our business. This is certainly true, and we do work hard to keep our best and brightest. But we look at it like this: Consider the impact to our business if we *didn't* invest in our staff. Would we want poorly trained team members to be our most loyal employees?

* * *

Change is the lifeblood of every company. Without change, there is no vitality, only stagnation. Every single change that is now taking place—in the world around you and in the people you serve and employ—represents an opening for you, as a leader, to step in and create something new. A new product or service. A new approach. A new attitude.

Change is the lifeblood of every company. Without change, there is no vitality, only stagnation.

Don't fear or avoid change. Lean into it. Love it. Leverage it.

BUT WAIT—BEFORE YOU GO!

Here are a few more thoughts about embracing change:

- Great processes are important. But obsession with *process* over results is a measure of a company that is not embracing change.

- Change requires investment. A big reason change often fails is that insufficient investment in the change is made by leadership.

- In most companies, employees become more set in their ways as time goes on, but in a company that repeatedly and successfully embraces change, employees actually become nimbler and more flexible as time goes on.

CHAPTER NINE

MAKING CHANGE HAPPEN

I often say to my leadership team, "We want the competition to be looking at our backside." By that I mean, of course, that *we* want to be the ones *leading* change, whenever possible.

If you don't change, you're standing still. And while you're standing still, your competition is evolving and improving, and your long-term competitive advantage can be lost. You end up *chasing* change instead of leading it.

Change entails a certain amount of discomfort; there's no way around it. Sometimes it seems that just when you finally get things running smoothly, you find yourself saying, "We need to evolve again." Why? Because when you look over your shoulder, you see that everyone's caught up to you and doing the same things you've been doing. Now you need to move forward again so they're always looking at your backside. You always want to be moving into areas where there's less competition, where you're not competing so fiercely on price, where you can charge a premium for your services and people are happy to pay it.

That kind of movement is tricky in an industry like ours, where everyone offers similar services. So for us it always comes down to culture being the differentiator. We're always looking to innovate with the *services* we offer, yes—but more than that, we're looking to innovate on the *way* we offer services. Because we think that's an area where we can be a field of one.

Find out where *you* can be a field of one, and start making the changes needed to get there.

CHARTING CHANGE

Change, by its nature, represents newness, something you've never done before. So by definition there's no universal formula for implementing change. That's part of why change makes people uncomfortable. It's always a bit of a journey into the unknown. But change *can* be planned in a thoughtful, methodical way.

First, you need to articulate a clear and organic reason for making the change. If you can't do that, then you're not ready to change. So it all starts with the objective. If you're going to change, that means you want to go from your current state, x, to something else, y. So what does your x state look like, and what do you think the y state will need to look like? Envision this clearly.

Again, change can be prompted for many reasons—the market, new technologies, new adjacencies you're trying to find. Change can occur because you want to shift from red-ocean strategies, where you're in high competition, to blue-ocean opportunities, where you hope to find yourself in a less cutthroat environment. Sometimes change involves a siloed process, where only one area of the company is involved; sometimes it involves a universal process that affects the entire company. It all comes down to a clear understanding of where you want to be once the change has taken place. Clarity about the "why" of the change is essential.

Next, you need to methodically break down all the parts of the process that will be affected. This is not unlike storyboarding a movie. It's all about process flow. Essentially what you're saying is, "Okay, here is where we want to end up, and here is where we are. Where are the asset gaps? The skills gaps? The resource gaps? The system gaps?" If your aim is to change processes or resources that are redundant, can the old resources be redeployed elsewhere?

Your approach to change is colored by the type, size, and age of your company. A young business can often afford to be more entrepreneurial and opportunistic in making changes. But if you're in a well-established, heavy-infrastructure business—like the automotive industry, for example—change can be difficult and expensive because of the huge costs required to set up your new processing ability. Smaller businesses and those in the service industry are nimbler, more able to adapt and change—provided your culture can embrace and execute on change opportunity. Change can occur on shorter timelines, and experimentation is possible.

SIZE MATTERS

The more mature you are as a company, the more thoughtful and comprehensive your approach to change needs to be. Seasons is a ten-year-old company, so we are now starting to look at change with a wider lens. As of this writing, we've set our objectives and goals for the upcoming year. And so we plan to sit down as an executive team and take a hard look at our current business resources in a fuller way than we've ever done before to make sure we have a complete understanding of where the gaps are, where we have redundancies, where we might realize some savings, and where we need to make investments.

Rather than simply being opportunistic and leveraging our entrepreneurial ability, we need to apply some rigor to our planning process to ensure we have a good talent plan in place. Since we plan to focus on new property development over the next few years, we will be asking ourselves, *Do we have the right team in place to be able to open three or four communities every year?* If not, what will that enhanced team need to look like? Can it be built from within the teams we already have? Or will we need to add to—or replace—some of the human resources we currently have?

Our comprehensive talent plan will need to include added steps for onboarding talent, retaining new and existing talent, and attracting talent to join the business going forward. It will need to ensure that we have sufficient talent for succession planning as well as for opening all the new communities we plan to open. These are considerations we didn't worry about so much when we were smaller and newer. So even your *approach to change* must itself change as your company grows! This is yet another level of change that must be orchestrated.

BEING A CHANGE AGENT

Being a great company leader includes being a skillful change agent. Not every leader possesses this skill—nor do you necessarily *want* every leader on your team to possess it. In some parts of your company, you need managers and executives who are simply good at keeping the engine running smoothly. But to thrive in changing times, there must be at least one person on your top leadership team, usually the CEO, who possesses the skills and mindset of a change agent.

As a change agent, your attitude must be one of *embracing* change. You must leverage change as a competitive tool rather than adapting to change only because you have to.

Of course being adaptive—nimble, responsive, flexible—is important as well. But being *strategic* about *why* you are adapting to a new technology, a new business model, or a new goal is doubly important. And strategy is where most leaders fall down. They tend to adapt late and to do so only because they've lost a competitive advantage and have no choice. As a result, they go into survival mode, and strategy goes out the window.

Survival mode is okay from time to time—provided you use it to transform yourself into a business that's better able to weather changing business conditions and take advantage of new opportunities. But the goal is to get out of survival mode as quickly as possible and shift into change-*leading* mode. I'm shocked by how often I hear leaders complaining about the disruptive effect of some new technology or business model that they "just can't compete effectively against." To me this attitude is astonishing. It's your job as a leader to not only *adapt* to change but to *anticipate* it and to find ways to use it to your company's advantage. You want to be the disrupt*or*, not the disrupt*ed*, whenever possible.

> It's your job as a leader to not only *adapt* to change but to *anticipate* it and to find ways to use it to your company's advantage.

INNOVATION MUST BE A CONSTANT

To be a change agent, you must build innovation into your company culture as well as into your personal job description. For me as a

CEO, that means I need to be spending 20 percent of my time—the equivalent of one workday per week—researching and developing ideas that are truly innovative. That includes exploring new ways of offering services, studying new developments in related industries, and uncovering hidden market opportunities that aren't being tapped. It also includes looking at new technologies that could help us work smarter, not harder. For example, we recently purchased a ride-on vacuum cleaner—I call it a carpet Zamboni—for one of our homes. It will allow us to reduce our maintenance man-hours but will also make the work more pleasant and effective. We might even try out an automated floor cleaner that requires no operator at all once programmed!

This constant drive to look outward for ways to change your business is an essential part of the forward-looking strategic mindset good businesses must possess.

YOU NEED TO BE "CHIEF SKEPTIC" TOO

Of course, not all change is good change or practical change. Part of your job as a change agent is to be the chief skeptic too.

I probably get ten phone calls or LinkedIn requests a week from people touting new services and technologies, saying, "Hey, give us a chunk of your time, open your books, and we'll tell you how we can improve your business." I could easily spend 70 percent of my workweek responding to requests like this, most of which would lead nowhere transformational.

And so there's some skepticism when anyone, including my team members and leaders, comes to me and says, "I think we should embed this piece of technology in our business" or suggests some other systemic change. My stance is usually a "show me" one. "How will we gain advantage from such a change?" I'll say. "What is the true investment for us? Who's going to be the champion for this change?"—because every change initiative needs a champion; someone who will become fluent in the new technology or process and help "sell" it to others. "What is the end goal—in specific and numerical terms, if possible—we hope to achieve? What are the true costs? And what are the costs if we *don't* do this?"

Only if such questions are answered in convincing fashion do we buckle down and start to build a road map for implementing the change.

Not even every *good* idea can be used. Change needs to occur at a rate that can be absorbed and internalized by your organization. If you throw too much change, too soon, at your workforce, you end up creating chaos and burnout. Part of your job as leader is to decide which changes have the most potential leverage to accomplish the greatest amount of long-term benefit. Those are the changes you should seek to implement.

CHIEF VISION OFFICER AND CHANGE EVANGELIST

As a leader, you need to really believe in any major change you're advocating, because ultimately you're going to be the one who sells it. If you haven't totally sold *yourself* on the idea, you won't be able to sell anyone else on it either. Your energy toward the idea must be such that it gets people excited enough to overcome their natural state of inertia.

It might be said that your job as CEO and change agent is to be the chief vision officer. Assuming your departmental leaders have been given the authority to run your day-to-day operations, that leaves you in charge of shareholder engagement. Your job is to sell messages like, "Here's where we need to go, folks. We want to get out of the red hypercompetitive zone we're in and take advantage of the competitive opportunities we see in this new area. If we go in this direction, we'll be in the blue zone—that differentiated space where we can be very profitable and won't be forced to commoditize our services. Our brand will stand out, new talent will be attracted to us, and customers will love us because our product is better than what they can get elsewhere. If we go in this direction, we can all be much more successful. Are you in?"

Your job as change agent is to be the evangelist, not just the process person. You need to be the one on the pulpit, the one telling the story again and again, the one communicating *why* you're making the change, the one creating the buy-in, the one engaging everyone and *keeping* them engaged via ongoing communication. People need to feel inspired if you want them to make changes and develop new habits and standards.

Again, in order to inspire others, you must BE the change you want to see in your company.

RESILIENCE IS ESSENTIAL

To be an effective change agent, you must be resilient. You're not always going to accomplish the changes you want *when* you want them or in the exact *way* you want them, so you must remain open and flexible and positive. Resilience is a quality I see lacking in many of today's upcoming leaders. They are often too willing to give up the vision too soon.

Resilience requires patience. You need to take the long view, not just look at the quarterly earnings reports and short-term metrics. Major change doesn't happen overnight; it happens incrementally. The ability to turn setbacks and short-term failures into positives is essential. Nobody responds to an "Eeyore." Remember Eeyore, the donkey character from the Winnie the Pooh stories who was able to find the black cloud in every situation? That type of negative energy needs to be completely eradicated. Resilience is the quality that empowers people to forge their way through periods of uncertainty and become great leaders that others want to follow and emulate. As things change around you, *you* must be the rock people can depend on. Your attitude must be the single constant that *doesn't* change, the light that is never dimmed. If you are not resilient, change will turn to chaos and disillusionment.

EFFECTING CHANGE

Change doesn't just happen. Wait, let me rephrase that. *Positive* change doesn't just happen. (Negative change, on the other hand, has a way of doing just fine on its own.) Change must be *led*, and it must be *managed*. When it comes to managing change, I find John Kotter's famous eight-step model of change management to be extremely useful. If you're not familiar with it, I encourage you to become so. I won't delve into it in this book, but I'll sum up the eight steps just for reference:

KOTTER'S EIGHT STEPS OF CHANGE

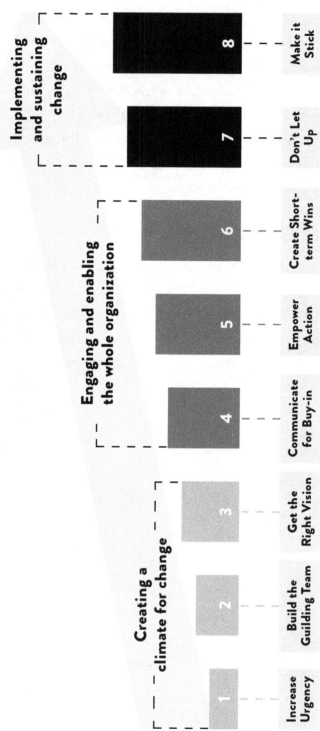

Creating a climate for change

1 — Increase Urgency

2 — Build the Guilding Team

3 — Get the Right Vision

Engaging and enabling the whole organization

4 — Communicate for Buy-in

5 — Empower Action

6 — Create Short-term Wins

Implementing and sustaining change

7 — Don't Let Up

8 — Make it Stick

Kotter's model provides a great basic framework for creating a specific change management plan that works within your particular organization. I use it and heartily endorse it.

Here are a few additional principles and methods I have discovered to be invaluable in my work as a change agent.

DON'T CLONE YOURSELF

One of the best ways to build change readiness into an organization is to create a dynamic team from the start. That means *not* hiring a bunch of you clones. Rather, hire people who are *not* like you—people who are smarter, older, younger, of different genders and backgrounds. As unnatural as it might seem, *don't* hire people who echo your point of view on everything. Because if you do, you will create an atmosphere of agreement, one in which everyone has the same basic perspective. That's the death of dynamic change.

Do hire people who share your overall vision, yes, but make sure they have their own ideas and approaches to add to the mix.

What you want is a variety of perspectives. You want team members who can see things you can't see from your own limited POV. You want people who know things you don't. Hiring this kind of person requires you to face your insecurities. You have to say to yourself, "Bringing aboard someone who has more knowledge than I have will likely make me feel uncomfortable." Yes, it will. Get over it. Comfort is not what you're looking for. Hiring people who are smarter than you and then giving them the reins to do their thing allows you to build a mentality of change, not stasis, into the very fabric of your organization.

START—STOP—CONTINUE

Establishing a current of constant, positive change in your workforce is challenging. In many companies, repetitive work habits tend to dictate employees' use of time. And very often these habits, which may have begun as productive ones, are no longer contributing true value.

At our company, we consider every minute of our time to be extremely valuable. And we believe we should be spending every one of those minutes on things that really contribute value to the organization, to our stakeholders, to our customers, and to ourselves as professionals. That's why we employ a process called Start—Stop—Continue.

Start—Stop—Continue simply means that you constantly and consciously evaluate how you are spending your time. You *stop* doing those things that are no longer contributing value—maybe they're just time fillers; maybe they're process problems; maybe they're legacy actions that once added value but no longer do. You *continue* doing those things that *are* contributing value in a clear and demonstrable way. And you *start* doing new things that you know *will* create value once you begin implementing them. Simple but powerful.

What this means is that everyone on your team should regularly be asking themselves, "Why are we doing this now? I know why we *started* doing this—to solve a problem—but has the problem gone away and we just forgot to stop doing the work?"

It's crucial to focus on NOW. What am I doing right this minute? Is it make-work, or is it the most valuable use of my time? Think, *I am a resource. My time is an investment. Are my current actions likely to lead to the highest returns on that investment?* We ask these questions once a month when we meet as an executive team. We also challenge each of our directors to ask them within their own business units every day. So in our accounting and finance department, for example, we're constantly asking, "Is there a more efficient way to do this task so that you could free up time to do some key analysis that will help us drive sales?" Same thing with our salespeople: "Are you spending too much time on clients who are obviously never going to convert? Are you still tapping the same mined-out referral sources, which are producing fewer and fewer prospects? Is it time to find new places to prospect for customers?"

When we look at what we're doing every day, we try to ask ourselves if we're employing the 80/20 principle in the right way. Are we spending 80 percent of our time on tasks that return only 20 percent of our value (bad)? Or are we focused on the 20 percent of tasks that can return 80 percent of our value (good)?

QUANTIFIABLE AND MEASURABLE

When it comes to change, numeric and quantifiable is the way to go. The more empirical and measurable your definition of a change can be, the more likely you will achieve the change you're hoping for. Numbers are simple, observable, unambiguous. Everyone can agree on them. On the other hand, a goal such as "We're going to improve our customer service in the upcoming year" is foggy and open to interpretation. Instead you should think about what "improved customer service" looks like numerically. Is it reducible to one key number? Does it entail several different factors? How can you track and measure them?

We believe there are two main metrics that are the most critical to our business when it comes to customer satisfaction. One is, "Would you refer someone you know to live here?" and the other is, "Do you have a strong sense that this is your home?" So we regularly ask our residents to rate their answers to these (and other) questions on a scale of one to five. On both of those questions, we recently scored 4.2 in our annual survey. That's a great indicator of the service our team is delivering to our people. But now that 4.2 will need to become a 4.3 for next year, and then a 4.4 the following year. Hard to achieve, but a concrete measurement—something we can all strive for and agree upon whether we hit our mark or not.

The same thing applies to growth. Why do we need to grow? Not just because that's what companies do. No, we need to grow because we're x percent less efficient than we can be. And if we can grow by y percent, our overhead will be spread across a larger revenue base, which means we will have z percent higher profitability. We work hard to establish those numbers in a concrete and meaningful way. That way, everyone knows the target. The more empirically we define our goals, the more likely we will achieve them.

When looking at areas of our company that we may want to change, we use a color-coded scheme—again, to make things more concrete and measurable. Every month in our executive meetings we make a large scorecard of the various parts of the business—sales, cash, human resources, staff retention, expenses, and so on. We then use red, amber, or green designations to label trends we see in each area and indicate whether they're heading in a positive direction, a negative direction, or a "watch and see" direction.

Being red is not necessarily a bad thing; there may be good reasons why a particular part of the company is not in growth mode at the moment. In some cases a red trend may indicate something that's out of our control, like taxes. But if we're always red, that means the process is flawed or we've adopted a technology that's just not working as we thought it would. Trends that are going in the wrong direction mean corrective action is required.

As our business matures, we gain a better sense of which areas are critical to growth and which are not. So at the beginning of the year, we might say, "Okay, these four things are prime indicators of success. If we can change these four reds into greens, that would really propel our business forward."

* * *

Businesses have a tendency to become insular over time. They become "addicted" to the ideas, processes, products, and systems that have gotten them to where they are today, and they forget that the world around them is changing. They forget that their business is about what the *customer* wants and that the customer is always evolving. Kodak was a classic example of this. It lulled itself into believing it was in the film business, when it was really in the business of preserving memories. Modern customers wanted to preserve their memories in ways that matched their changing technological lifestyles. That meant going digital. Kodak didn't change.

If you always ask yourself, "What is the true value I am providing to customers?" you'll find the answer is always bigger than the particular products, technologies, and services you are offering at any given moment. At Seasons, for example, we're in the business of creating living spaces that feel like home. And as the concept of "home" continues to change and evolve for people, we'll need to change to keep up with it.

BUT WAIT—BEFORE YOU GO!

Here are some final thoughts about making change happen:

- People only desire to change when they're in sufficient pain or when they see a promise of something better. Your job as change agent is to sell that promise of something better.

- You can't solve a problem with the same mindset that created the problem. Bringing in a fresh point of view may be essential.

- Change is risk. Having a good risk management plan in place makes change more palatable.

CHAPTER TEN

CREATING A CULTURE OF CHANGE

I f you've been in business more than five minutes, you have probably heard Peter Drucker's famous quote, which I referred to earlier: "Culture eats strategy for breakfast." And yet many—if not most—leadership teams spend the bulk of their time talking about strategy while culture remains a bit of an afterthought.

Strategy is important, but ultimately it has no power to motivate and execute. Execution is carried out by flesh-and-blood human beings. And if those human beings are not steeped in a culture of change, then good luck executing that brilliant new strategy!

A great culture, almost by definition, is a dynamic one. That means it is responsive, flexible, and adaptable, not stale, formal, and stodgy. Dynamic culture lives in the present moment, not in "the way we've always done things." It is ever ready to change in response to shifting business needs, emerging technologies, and new customers with new preferences.

A dynamic culture never views itself as "finished"; it is always in a state of evolvement. It welcomes new ideas and is open to experimentation and creative failure. It learns by *trying* new things, not by sitting back and abstractly analyzing. And it has fun while doing it.

In a dynamic culture, ideas can come from anywhere—top, middle, or bottom. And there's no blame if the idea doesn't pan out.

Here is a simple example ...

SUPERWATER

We were recently having one of our "internal trade shows," where we get together to discuss current and emerging practices in our various departments. This particular meeting involved our environmental services managers. One of our guys came forward and said, "Hey, I have a friend who's selling this new product. It's basically ozonated water. You put regular water through some sort of chemical/electrical process and turn it from O_2 into O_3. And when it's in O_3 form, it has amazing cleaning properties. It's antibacterial and antiviral—comparable to 20 percent ethyl alcohol when you rub it on surfaces. It's relatively inexpensive, and after twenty-four hours the O_3 goes back to O_2! That means it's odorless and leaves no residuals. So it's great from a hazmat perspective and super safe for employees. I think we should give it a shot."

We said, "Sounds like a great idea. Do you mind being the test home and point person for this?" He said sure, so we looked into it a bit more. The product seemed legit, so we had the company come in and do a test installation. We liked what we saw. There was very little risk to employees in using it or misusing it—after all, the stuff was just water. So from a chemical perspective, it was great for everyone. In practical terms, it was soft on materials, so it didn't corrode any of our surfaces. It was good on glass, good on sinks, good on toilets. So we also reduced the total number of chemicals we had to carry on our cleaning carts. In short, we tried it, it was working, and we loved it.

We were on the way to incorporating it system-wide when we had an inspection from our public health people, and they said, "We like what you're doing with this product, and we know they're using it in hospitals. The problem is, ozonated water doesn't have a DIN." A DIN, or drug and chemical identification number, is required by the Public Health Agency of Canada. "Although we all sense intuitively that this stuff has great benefits, we can't approve it because it hasn't been stringently lab tested and we don't know its true efficacy and safety."

So we went back to the manufacturer and told them what had happened, and they said, "Yeah, we've been going through the approval process, but they're not making it easy for us."

Our reply was, "Okay, but in our setting, we're caring for vulnerable people who do tend to get sick, and when there are outbreaks, public health folks tend to scrutinize us pretty carefully. So, for now, we're going to have to discontinue using the product. If and when conditions change, give us a shout."

So this was a great idea, one that we were glad our team member brought forward. We adopted it. We tested it. We worked through some of the kinks with it. And then we had to let it go because it didn't quite fit all the criteria needed to keep all our stakeholders happy.

This is a simple example of how we are perfectly prepared to try something new but also perfectly willing and able to say, "Nope. Not working out, guys. Got to change course."

This sort of thing happens several times a year in our organization, and we've found some great new products, technologies, and solutions this way. The ability to openly play with new ideas—

whether they're bottom-up ideas or top-down ideas—is not as easy as it sounds. Many organizations just don't have the nimbleness to say, "Let's give this thing a shot" and to have their team members try it with enthusiasm, creativity, and accountability.

For that you need a dynamic culture.

WHAT IS A DYNAMIC CULTURE?

A dynamic culture is one that is alive and vibrant. It is focused on the present and the future, not the past. You can see, feel, and taste a dynamic culture when you walk in the door of a business. There's an energy and a "ready for business" vibration in the air. You can see it in the energetic way the leadership team and the staff interact with each other. You can see it in the way tasks are organized—there's a process in place that's geared for success. You can see it in the demeanor of the staff; they're smiling and having fun, but they also seem organized. You can see it in the way managers and staff interact with their customers; they look happy to take care of them and eager to interact with them as the moment demands.

I'll give you a simple example of the latter. I recently stayed in a Marriott hotel on vacation. I was walking toward an elevator that required a key card to access my floor. I had two coffees in my hands, so in order to use the keycard, I was going to have to either stack the coffees under my chin or put one of them down. No big deal, but a bit of a hassle.

The concierge in the lobby took one look at where I was headed and said, "Just a second, let me help you." He hurried over to the elevator ahead of me, put his keycard in the slot, said, "Which floor are you going to?" and pressed the button for me. He anticipated my needs without my asking for help. It cost him nothing to help me. And I wouldn't have faulted him had he not obliged. But his simple act made me feel cared for and attended to—and now I'm including it in this book! This is a great example of someone who was living their culture and knew what their job was and how to execute it.

A dynamic culture permeates an organization and is built on a foundation of people understanding what their job is, receiving excellent training, and then being given enough latitude to unleash their enthusiasm on customers.

CULTURE IS WHAT HAPPENS WHEN YOU'RE NOT LOOKING

If I had to define culture, I would say it is a collection of behaviors and attitudes that speak to a common understanding of what success is. But culture, good or bad, has a life of its own. Another way of saying this is that culture is what happens when you're not looking.

A true measure of a great and dynamic culture is that it continues to do your work *for* you, in positive ways, after you leave the room. It advances your company goals even when you're not telling it to.

This plays out in measurable and observable ways across many aspects of an organization. You can see it in the way the staff interacts. As I've mentioned before, a great culture is self-policing. Its members don't tolerate sloppy attitudes or lack of accountability, and they speak up whenever they see coworkers slacking. When self-policing starts to happen in a company, your need for disciplinary action goes down and your staff retention goes up.

> A dynamic culture permeates an organization and is built on a foundation of people understanding what their job is, receiving excellent training, and then being given enough latitude to unleash their enthusiasm on customers.

You can see it in the way staff members interact with customers. They form genuine relationships with each other, in ways that have nothing to do with you. Employees spontaneously do thoughtful and *personal* things for customers. Mutual affection is evident, and there is a warm tolerance for staff mistakes when they happen. As a result, complaints about staff go way down. Customers are so happy with the service they're receiving that they begin referring friends and relatives. Sales go up without any direct effort on your part.

You can see it in the way employees behave even when they're not at work. They "advertise" their connection to the company by wearing the company "swag"—sweatshirts and hats with the company logo, that sort of thing. And when they're out in the community or among friends and family, they're eager to talk about the company. They rave about how they love working there, and as a result, you get a wealth of great talent knocking on HR's door without your needing to do aggressive recruiting.

All the strategy in the world can't accomplish these kinds of things.

A GREAT CULTURE DOESN'T RUN ON FEAR

Another measure of a dynamic culture is that it is risk tolerant rather than fearful and risk averse. That means employees are willing to try new things that aren't in the employee handbook. They are willing to step forward with innovative ideas, because they know they won't be crucified if the idea ultimately fails or is passed over.

A lot goes into creating a culture that is risk tolerant. First of all, there must be a high level of trust in the management—trust that if my idea is used, the credit for it won't be stolen; trust that if the idea is tried and fails, my boss won't throw me under the bus. So that means the whole management team must be operating from a position of strong ethics. Also, there needs to be a level of caring and connectedness among employees, so that when a person's ideas *are* tried, they receive the earnest support and effort of their teammates.

When a culture is risk tolerant, it is willing to experiment and to learn from failures, as in the case of the O_3 trial mentioned earlier. Here's another quick example:

Recently a member of our management team proposed using a new kind of carpeting in our suites. The kind we had been using—a residential-looking Berber—was cost effective to buy, but we were finding it was basically disposable. Almost every time we turned a suite over, we had to replace it. So we weren't getting a lot of life cycle value out of it. The proposed new product was more expensive but more durable. We had some healthy debate, back and forth, about adopting it. Some folks were in favor of the new carpeting; some were in favor of the old.

So we said, "Here's what we're going to do. We're going to negotiate the best price we can and commit to a hundred thousand square feet of the new carpet a year for three years. Then, at the end of three years, we'll reevaluate. If we're getting better results and savings with the new carpeting, great—it's a win. If it turns out the old carpeting was better after all, that's also a win. We can go back to using that carpeting with renewed confidence."

By treating the decision like an experiment, everyone felt heard and went away happy, feeling that the best solution would simply make itself evident over time. It's wonderful to be part of a culture where everyone feels like they're on the same side and you can freely experiment without putting the burden of success or failure on any one individual's head.

CREATING A DYNAMIC CULTURE

Culture happens whether you want it to or not. The only question is whether you are going to get out ahead of it and consciously create the culture you want or sit back and say, "I didn't see *that* coming" when things go horribly wrong. At Seasons, culture is job one. It is our reason for existing, it is our profit engine, and it is our daily focus. We know that organizations, by their nature, are resistant to change and that only if you make dynamic change a *feature* of your culture can you hope to have a workforce that adapts to new ideas with energy and positivity. Here are a few ways we try to do that at Seasons …

"INTERNAL TRADE SHOWS"

I've talked about the Start—Stop—Continue approach we use in our executive team meetings and our departments. One way we make Start—Stop—Continue a tangible reality is by hosting the "internal trade shows" I've mentioned. At least twice a year, we bring our service leaders together by discipline and review our practices to see how they're working. We also bring in outside vendors and experts with new ideas and products. So for our dining team, for example, we might walk them through a tasting menu presented by our food suppliers. Maybe some seafood experts will come in and our staff will try some new recipes. Or maybe we'll invite a vendor in to demonstrate a new technology, like that high-tech oven I've referred to.

We'll also sit down with our teams and talk about some of the challenges they're facing, whether that's with staffing, onboarding, public health compliance, equipment, or whatever. And we'll have some of our most successful people share their best practices with everyone as well—such as how to grow organic herbs or creative ways to use leftovers.

With our environmental people, perhaps we'll take them on-site to one of our new buildings and bring in some of our outside consultants, such as our HVAC specialists. They'll walk everyone through the equipment rooms and the maintenance procedures, showing off their latest stuff. Then we'll gather everyone around a table to see what new ideas come to light.

Same thing for our nurses and housekeepers. We'll talk about our current practices, and we'll look at some new options as well, all with a Start—Stop—Continue mentality; that is, should we stop what we're doing, continue what we're doing, or try something new?

When people get out of their everyday work environments and literally taste, touch, and see new ideas at work, they get *excited* about making changes rather than resistant to them.

ENGAGEMENT AND FEEDBACK

At Seasons, we try, whenever possible, to actively engage our staff in decision-making, especially when a proposed change affects them directly. For example, I spoke earlier about a time when we were trying to come up with a uniform for our staff.

First we engaged the staff in a lively conversation about whether it would be better for the staff to wear one uniform or to wear different uniforms by department. Once we came to an agreement that staff should wear a single uniform, we had a second conversation about color. The team narrowed it down to three possibilities: white, blue, or black, and we discussed the pros and cons of each, at length. Then we put it to a vote. Black won.

Next we said, "Okay, so we're going to try some pants and shirts from a few different vendors. You're going to wear them for a while and tell us how you like them." And so we did that, and we collected the feedback. Eventually we came up with a uniform that not only works for our brand (noninstitutional, sharp, professional, accessible) but also has the buy-in of the staff. Why? Because they were actively engaged in the selection process and in providing feedback.

Of course, with 1,500 employees, we couldn't engage every single person, but we did engage a good representative sample. When people are actively involved in the change process, they don't feel as if change is something that's being foisted upon them and that their only option is to go along; they feel like part of the change process. They *own* the change.

HELPING EMPLOYEES BE SUCCESSFUL

One of the best ways to promote a dynamic, change-ready culture is to help people feel successful at what they're doing. When employees see that your company's approach works, and they feel like a successful part of it, they develop trust in the company and the culture, and they want to be part of it as it evolves going forward. They also feel greater satisfaction in their jobs. Helping employees feel successful means giving them the right tools. For example …

GOOD ONBOARDING AND TRAINING

We talked earlier about how seriously we take the job of onboarding. Typically, a service-team leader at Seasons is not even allowed to do their job alone for the first two weeks of their employment. Many companies take the attitude, "Here's the pool—jump in and learn to swim." Our attitude is, "Here's the pool. Here's the way it works. Here's the temperature we keep it at. Here's the way you'll feel in the water. Here's how to get in and out safely. Here's the team that maintains the pool. Here's where you go for help with the pool

..." You get the idea. We connect the dots so each person has a firm understanding of where they fit in the wider web. And we continue to expose them to more and more aspects of the organization the longer they stay with us.

HEART

We also give people permission to make mistakes. We tell them, "There are times when you won't be successful despite your best efforts, and that's okay. When you don't succeed with a client, here's what you do." And we teach them the HEART approach:

- Hear what the client has to say. Listen to their complaint without interrupting or justifying the staff's behavior.

- Empathize with the client—say something like, "I can see why you're feeling upset." Then ...

- Apologize sincerely. Once you've said you're sorry, they can't carry on complaining, because you've acknowledged their bad experience. Then attempt to ...

- Resolve the issue by proposing an action step, such as, "Let's you and I go together to the nursing department and bring this issue up to them." And finally ...

- Thank the person for sharing their concern, because that is how the process—and the company—gets refined and improved.

Permission to make mistakes takes the fear out of trying something new.

A SHARED CULTURAL LANGUAGE

To create a tight culture, it's important to have some sort of shared language. Language is the common thread that helps people understand what they do and why they do it. If you don't have a shared language to describe what you're up to, everyone starts using their own words, and pretty soon your shared mission starts to sound like a bunch of different missions.

Some companies—like the Googles and Apples—are almost cultish in the language they use. They have acronyms and special terms for everything. That's okay in some environments, but in ours we try to strike a balance. We use *some* Seasons-specific terminology—such as Connect, Care, Change—but we try to keep our day-to-day speech as plain as possible because we don't want it to sound like a foreign language to our customers. That would only serve to distance us from customers.

At the same time, we want to make sure we're all using language that's uniformly appropriate and doesn't make our customers feel patronized. It's important that our language conveys to each customer that they are special and that we have a caring and deep relationship with them.

For that reason, we frown upon a common practice in our industry, which is to call residents *Dear* or *Sweetie* or *Honey*. First of all, it's condescending. Second, in most cases the resident has not given us permission to refer to them that way. Third, there's nothing special or individualized about such terms. You're using one word to address every resident.

We prefer that staff members ask permission to call residents by their first name. Usually the resident says yes, but if they say no, then we call them Mrs. Smith or Mr. Wiggins. And if a resident says, "Call me Millie; only my mother calls me Mildred," even better. Now you've created a special relationship with that resident. But don't call her Sweetie.

Even more important than a shared language is a shared *understanding*. That's why it's vital to have transparency throughout an organization. Be open about any major changes you're considering. Explain to people why the change is being considered and what you hope to gain by effecting the change. Solicit feedback from folks, get them involved in the change, and help them understand the role they will play as change occurs.

OVERCOMING RESISTANCE TO CHANGE

Even in the most dynamic of cultures, there will be pockets of resistance to change. The best way to deal with resistance is to actively flush it out and deal with it in a forthright manner.

IDENTIFY THE ANXIETY

People resist change largely because of anxiety. Sometimes they are not even aware of where their own anxieties lie. They may claim to be resistant to the change for seemingly logical reasons, but the deeper reason is that the change feels personally threatening to them on some level.

As a leader, it is wise to try to understand the true source of any resistance to change because, as I've said before, people are anxiety-reducing machines. They'll do whatever it takes to make anxiety go away, even if that means sabotaging a change that might be good for them and for the company. So engage in authentic conversations, identify the anxiety, and address it honestly, whether it's unwarranted or in fact has some basis in reality.

ROOT OUT ANCHORED POSITIONS

Another reason people resist change is that they have an anchored position—something they just don't want to budge on. Often, as with anxieties, they don't openly acknowledge the true reason for their anchored position. You are led to believe they're objecting to the change for one reason, but the true reason lies elsewhere.

For instance, when we were doing the carpet experiment above, an environmental guy in one of our homes was really not a fan of the new product. He kept digging in his heels, coming up with reason after reason why the product wasn't performing. It got to the point where we called the manufacturer and asked them to send a rep to one of our internal trade shows.

The carpet rep showed up and asked our resistant employee, "What's your biggest problem with our carpet?" The employee said, "Gum." So the rep threw down some gum on the new carpet and pressed it in with his heel. He then showed everyone how easy it was to remove.

Our employee then said urine on the carpet was a huge issue. Thankfully, the rep didn't urinate on the carpet, but he did come up with a liquid containing proteins that were difficult to remove. He let it sit for a while and then he cleaned it up without much effort.

Next our guy said, "Well, it's really hard to vacuum." And the rep proceeded to throw some potting soil on the carpet and grind it in. He then demonstrated the correct way to vacuum it. "It's easy if you work in the direction of the nap. It's just *push forward and pull back slowly.*"

Our environmental guy finally ran out of arguments, and the true reason for his objections finally came to light. It turned out his local carpet installer, who was sort of a friend, was now being cut out of the loop. He was still doing installations for us, but he was no longer able to make a markup on the product itself because we had prenegotiated the price with the distributor. So we had shaved his profit margins. *Sorry, but that's not really our problem.*

By taking our employee's objections at face value and logically eliminating them one by one, we were able to root out his true anchored position. In the process, we were able to demonstrate to the other team members why we had chosen the new product, and they walked away more sold on it than ever.

DEAL WITH THE ENERGY VAMPIRES

In every organization, there are culture drainers—people whose negative attitudes can sabotage a culture if they're not dealt with. Often they smile to your face and put on a good show at meetings, but behind your back, they sap positivity. We call these people "energy vampires." Again, rooting them out and addressing the problem head-on is the only course.

At our company we have a couple of advantages in this fight. First, because our culture tends to be self-policing, our people don't put up with the energy vampires. They deal with them directly, and if that doesn't work, they bring them to management's attention. A second advantage is that we spend a lot of time up front getting buy-in from the people we hire. We make it crystal clear what our expectations are, so if there's a problem later on, we can say, "Remember when we hired you, we said there were some things that were nonnegotiable? I'm not sure your recent performance is in keeping with what we established as our shared understanding of what success looks like. How are we going to get back on track?"

Because we have a relationship-based culture, we're usually able to spot such slippages before they go too far, and we're connected enough to our employees that we're able to have open, authentic conversations with them.

* * *

Authentic conversations. Remember that topic? We started the book with it, and it's fitting we should end with it as well. Authenticity is the heart of every great service culture. Without it, you're just going through the motions. Connections are shallow, Caring is reduced to phony smiles and transactional exchanges, and no one wants to Change for you. Authenticity simply means putting the real you into everything you do.

If there is only one thing you remember from this book, I hope it is this: Business is a *human* enterprise. It is nothing more or less than the people involved in it—the employees, the customers, the vendors, the stakeholders. Job one for any manager or leader is to build relationships and to keep them vital and healthy. Everything else is secondary.

Build a culture based on authentic relationships, and you will have a team that follows you to the ends of the earth. Fail to do so, and all the business-school tricks in the world won't get you anywhere.

Connect.

Care.

Change.

Triumph.

BUT WAIT—BEFORE YOU GO!

Here are a few more thoughts about creating a dynamic culture:

- A great culture must be based on a handful of simple but powerful ideas that everyone *gets* and can rally behind. If it takes you a page and a half to define your culture, it's too complicated.

- Signs of a great culture: laughter, camaraderie, teamwork, people being valued, a shared dream, good ethics, mutual respect, orderliness, show readiness. Signs of a poor culture: blame, authority as a main management tool, complaining, backbiting, risk aversity, low energy, messiness.

- A strong culture can propel you forward, but it can also hold you back—if it is mired in ideas from the past. Blockbuster Video seemed to have a strong culture, but it was married to the idea of brick-and-mortar video stores. Netflix ate it for lunch. *Change* must be engrained in the culture.

- Change can't happen without the other two Cs. If you don't Connect with people and Care about them, you can't possibly know what they want or need, so you can't effect Change within them or around them. Change is inseparable from Connecting and Caring.

Printed in the USA
CPSIA information can be obtained
at www.ICGtesting.com
JSHW012031140824
68134JS00033B/2997